Tom Lansford, editor

Conflict resolution: opposing
  viewpoints

Conflict Resolution

Other Books of Related Interest:

At Issues Series

How Should the U.S. Proceed in Iraq?

Should Governments Negotiate with Terrorists?

United Nations

Opposing Viewpoints Series

Legal System

"Congress shall make no law ... abridging the freedom of speech, or of the press."

First Amendment to the U.S. Constitution

The basic foundation of our democracy is the First Amendment guarantee of freedom of expression. The Opposing Viewpoints Series is dedicated to the concept of this basic freedom and the idea that it is more important to practice it than to enshrine it.

OPPOSING VIEWPOINTS® SERIES

Conflict Resolution

Tom Lansford, Book Editor

WITHDRAWN

GREENHAVEN PRESS
A part of Gale, Cengage Learning

GALE
CENGAGE Learning™

Detroit • New York • San Francisco • New Haven, Conn • Waterville, Maine • London

Christine Nasso, *Publisher*
Elizabeth Des Chenes, *Managing Editor*

For more information, contact:
Greenhaven Press
27500 Drake Rd.
Farmington Hills, MI 48331-3535
Or you can visit our Internet site at gale.cengage.com

For product information and technology assistance, contact us at

Gale Customer Support, 1-800-877-4253
For permission to use material from this text or product, submit all requests online at
www.cengage.com/permissions

Further permissions questions can be emailed to permissionrequest@cengage.com

Articles in Greenhaven Press anthologies are often edited for length to meet page require-
ments. In addition, original titles of these works are changed to clearly present the main
thesis and to explicitly indicate the author's opinion. Every effort is made to ensure that
Greenhaven Press accurately reflects the original intent of the authors. Every effort has
been made to trace the owners of copyrighted material.

Cover photograph reproduced by permission of Image200/Images.com/Getty Images.

LIBRARY OF CONGRESS CATALOGING-IN-PUBLICATION DATA

Conflict resolution / Tom Lansford, book editor.
   p. cm. -- (Opposing viewpoints)
   Includes bibliographical references and index.
   ISBN-13: 978-0-7377-3992-3 (hardcover)
   ISBN-13: 978-0-7377-3993-0 (pbk.)
   1. Conflict management. I. Lansford, Tom.
   HM1126.C648 2008
   303.6'9--dc22

                               2008014670

Printed in the United States of America
1 2 3 4 5 6 7 12 11 10 09 08

Contents

Chapter 3: Is Conflict Resolution the Best Way to Solve Environmental Problems?

Why Consider Opposing Viewpoints?

> *"The only way in which a human being can make some approach to knowing the whole of a subject is by hearing what can be said about it by persons of every variety of opinion and studying all modes in which it can be looked at by every character of mind. No wise man ever acquired his wisdom in any mode but this."*
>
> *John Stuart Mill*

In our media-intensive culture it is not difficult to find differing opinions. Thousands of newspapers and magazines and dozens of radio and television talk shows resound with differing points of view. The difficulty lies in deciding which opinion to agree with and which "experts" seem the most credible. The more inundated we become with differing opinions and claims, the more essential it is to hone critical reading and thinking skills to evaluate these ideas. Opposing Viewpoints books address this problem directly by presenting stimulating debates that can be used to enhance and teach these skills. The varied opinions contained in each book examine many different aspects of a single issue. While examining these conveniently edited opposing views, readers can develop critical thinking skills such as the ability to compare and contrast authors' credibility, facts, argumentation styles, use of persuasive techniques, and other stylistic tools. In short, the Opposing Viewpoints Series is an ideal way to attain the higher-level thinking and reading skills so essential in a culture of diverse and contradictory opinions.

In addition to providing a tool for critical thinking, Opposing Viewpoints books challenge readers to question their own strongly held opinions and assumptions. Most people form their opinions on the basis of upbringing, peer pressure, and personal, cultural, or professional bias. By reading carefully balanced opposing views, readers must directly confront new ideas as well as the opinions of those with whom they disagree. This is not to simplistically argue that everyone who reads opposing views will—or should—change his or her opinion. Instead, the series enhances readers' understanding of their own views by encouraging confrontation with opposing ideas. Careful examination of others' views can lead to the readers' understanding of the logical inconsistencies in their own opinions, perspective on why they hold an opinion, and the consideration of the possibility that their opinion requires further evaluation.

Evaluating Other Opinions

To ensure that this type of examination occurs, Opposing Viewpoints books present all types of opinions. Prominent spokespeople on different sides of each issue as well as well-known professionals from many disciplines challenge the reader. An additional goal of the series is to provide a forum for other, less known, or even unpopular viewpoints. The opinion of an ordinary person who has had to make the decision to cut off life support from a terminally ill relative, for example, may be just as valuable and provide just as much insight as a medical ethicist's professional opinion. The editors have two additional purposes in including these less known views. One, the editors encourage readers to respect others' opinions—even when not enhanced by professional credibility. It is only by reading or listening to and objectively evaluating others' ideas that one can determine whether they are worthy of consideration. Two, the inclusion of such viewpoints encourages the important critical thinking skill of objectively evaluating an author's credentials and bias. This evaluation will illuminate an author's reasons for taking a particular stance on an issue and will aid in readers' evaluation of the author's ideas.

It is our hope that these books will give readers a deeper understanding of the issues debated and an appreciation of the complexity of even seemingly simple issues when good and honest people disagree. This awareness is particularly important in a democratic society such as ours in which people enter into public debate to determine the common good. Those with whom one disagrees should not be regarded as enemies but rather as people whose views deserve careful examination and may shed light on one's own.

Thomas Jefferson once said that "difference of opinion leads to inquiry, and inquiry to truth." Jefferson, a broadly educated man, argued that "if a nation expects to be ignorant and free . . . it expects what never was and never will be." As individuals and as a nation, it is imperative that we consider the opinions of others and examine them with skill and discernment. The Opposing Viewpoints Series is intended to help readers achieve this goal.

David L. Bender and Bruno Leone,
Founders

Introduction

"The world will look to Washington for more than rhetoric the next time we face a challenge to peace."

American diplomat
Richard Holbrooke

On March 5, 1992, Bosnia declared its independence from the former Yugoslavia following a referendum in which the population voted overwhelmingly—99 percent—in favor of establishing a new country. Bosnia was one of six countries in the Yugoslav federation that included Croatia, Macedonia, Montenegro, Serbia, and Slovenia. Croatia and Slovenia had already declared independence, but the central government of the former Yugoslavia was determined to prevent other states from leaving the federation. Bosnia had a mixed population that included large numbers of ethnic Bosnians, Croats, and Serbs. Bosnians made up the majority of the population, 43 percent, followed by the Serbs, with 31 percent, and the Croats, with 17 percent. After independence, a broad ethnic conflict broke out among the different groups within Bosnia. Supported by the government of the former Yugoslavia, ethnic Serbs attempted to take control of the new country and become part of Serbia. Meanwhile, the government of the newly independent Croatia, supported Croat forces. Sporadic fighting began almost immediately after independence was declared.

The Cold War superpower conflict between the United States and the Soviet Union had just ended, and American political leaders hoped that the growing dispute could be resolved through conflict resolution, rather than military action. The administrations of Presidents George H.W. Bush and Bill

Clinton signaled their support for European states, including France, Germany, and the United Kingdom, to take the lead in containing the conflict. Meanwhile, U.S. military forces that had been stationed in Europe during the Cold War were beginning to be redeployed. Through the early 1990s, the United States reduced its troop strength in Europe by more than three hundred thousand soldiers.

The international community undertook a range of attempts at conflict resolution in an effort to prevent the escalation of strife. The European Community (EC) immediately launched a peace conference and endorsed a plan developed by British politician Lord Peter Carrington and Portuguese ambassador José Cutileiro in September 1992. The Carrington-Cutileiro peace plan called for the major ethnic groups in Bosnia to share political and economic power. However, many in the global community feared that the EC plan might not work since the major world powers did not offer a high degree of public support. Many also argued that any resolution of the conflict would require the backing of the North Atlantic Treaty Organization (NATO), a Western military alliance that was formed during the Cold War and included all of the main European and North American allies, such as the United States, Canada, France, Germany, Italy, and the United Kingdom. The EC plan did not include a role for NATO. This reflected the uncertainty of the continuing U.S. role in European security. British prime minister John Major declared that "NATO, the EC and America were all unsure of their international roles." This ambiguity about the role of the most powerful country in the world at the time would hurt efforts at conflict resolution in Bosnia.

Meanwhile, the United Nations (UN) Security Council adopted Resolution 713, which imposed an arms embargo on Bosnia so as to prevent weapons from flowing to the country. However, both of these initiatives failed to stop the spread of violence. Although they initially agreed to the Carrington-

Cutileiro plan, the Bosnians, Croats, and Serbs soon withdrew from the accords because of suspicion and mistrust. In addition, the Serbs gained control of most of the weapons of the former Yugoslav army, and both the ethnic Serbs and Croats received weapons from their home countries, so that the UN embargo hurt mainly the Bosnians.

Wide-scale fighting began in the winter of 1992–1993. The Serbs, supported by the Yugoslav army, captured most of the territory in eastern Bosnia and eventually controlled 70 percent of Bosnia. They then launched an effort to force ethnic Bosnians and Croats from their homes. This strategy was designed to solidify Serb control over the area and came to be known as "ethnic cleansing." In many instances, civilians were murdered as forces attempted to remove people from their homes. During the fighting, all of the groups engaged in ethnic cleansing to some extent, but the majority of the atrocities were committed by ethnic Serbs. The civil war killed more than 250,000 people and created more than 1.3 million refugees.

In response to the loss of life and the spread of civil war, the United Nations approved the deployment of a peacekeeping force, known as the UN Protection Force, or UNPROFOR. It was hoped that the UN soldiers could stabilize the country while negotiations ended the fighting. A new plan to resolve the civil war was developed by former U.S. secretary of state Cyrus Vance and EC diplomat Lord David Owen. Unfortunately, the Serbs rejected the Vance-Owen plan because it would have required that they surrender much of the territory they had recently conquered. In an effort to increase pressure on Serbia to negotiate, the UN adopted a "no-fly" zone over Bosnia. This measure forbade military aircraft from flying over the region. It was enforced by NATO warplanes. On February 28, 1994, NATO aircraft shot down four Serbian warplanes.

Serb attacks on the Bosnian capital of Sarajevo caused widespread civilian casualties. International reporters and television crews broadcast images of the slaughter around the world, prompting increasing pressure to end the fighting. In response to the attacks, NATO conducted air strikes on Serb military targets around Sarajevo, beginning on August 30, 1995. These attacks convinced the Serbs to negotiate.

Representatives of the United States, the European Community, Bosnia, Croatia, and Serbia met in Dayton, Ohio, and crafted the Dayton Peace Accords, which was signed on November 21, 1995. This agreement divided Bosnia into two broad areas, the Bosnian-Croat Federation and the Republic of Serbia. The Federation and the Republic each was given roughly half of Bosnia's territory (the Bosnian-Croat Federation received 51 percent of the land, and the Serbs, 49 percent). In addition to these entities, a single, overarching government was created, led by a president. The presidency rotates among the three main ethnic groups every three months. The accords also paved the way for a large, NATO-led peacekeeping force of sixty thousand troops. Although the NATO mission is now over, international peacekeepers remain in Bosnia as of 2008.

The Dayton accords were widely praised by many. U.S. president Bill Clinton called the agreement a "victory for all those who believe in a multi-ethnic democracy in Bosnia." But others in the United States and around the world argued that the international community acted too late. They contend that the United States and the EC should have done more to promote conflict resolution before the fighting became widespread. In addition, a little more than three years later, fighting broke out again, this time in the former Yugoslav Republic of Serbia, in the province of Kosovo. Republican senator Trent Lott of Mississippi declared that in the Kosovo crisis "I didn't think we [the United States] had done enough in the diplomatic area." His sentiments reflected the failure of the United

States to support international efforts to resolve conflicts before they escalated. Nonetheless Clinton used the Bosnian crisis to argue for a more forceful role for the United States during times of civil war. He declared in 1999 that the United States "can say to the people of the world, whether you live in Africa, or Central Europe, or any other place, if somebody comes after innocent civilians and tries to kill them en masse because of their race, their ethnic background or their religion, and it's within our power to stop it, we will stop it."

People throughout the world increasingly seek alternative strategies to end violence. Conflict resolution techniques and programs offer a range of alternatives to force or traditional legal means of reducing violence. From the school playground to the courtroom to the international arena, conflict resolution provides different approaches to prevent strife or to end disputes before they escalate. The authors in *Opposing Viewpoints: Conflict Resolution* examine the issues surrounding dispute resolution. The contributors explore four main themes: How should conflict resolution be taught? Is conflict resolution a good alternative to legal action? Are conflict resolution strategies the best way to solve environmental problems? and What methods are effective in resolving international conflicts? Conflict resolution has shown great promise in a number of areas, but it is also subject to criticism and doubt. One area in which most people agree is the importance of the individual in resolving disputes. As the American philosopher William James noted: "Whenever you're in conflict with someone, there is one factor that can make the difference between damaging your relationship and deepening it. That factor is attitude."

How Should Conflict Resolution Be Taught?

Chapter Preface

School violence has become an increasing problem in the United States. Two of the most notable incidents are the 1999 shooting at Colorado's Columbine High School, in which twelve students and one teacher were killed and twenty-three others were wounded, and the 2007 Virginia Tech massacre, in which thirty-three students and professors died. The scholar Alixandra Blitz summarized perceptions about school violence when she wrote, "Students have always fought on the playground, engaged in fistfights, stole property, and quarreled over friendships. However, since the early 1990s, American schools have faced heightened levels of violence."

In an effort to prevent such attacks, as well as address bullying and harassment, more and more schools have embraced conflict resolution and alternative dispute resolution strategies. Many of these techniques were developed in the 1960s and 1970s, but became increasingly popular in the 1990s. However, by the 2000s, critics asserted that contemporary education programs on conflict resolution were ineffective and needed to be reevaluated. One area of debate has revolved around when conflict resolution education should begin. Many experts have asserted that children should be exposed to conflict resolution tactics at very young ages, but others have argued that such education is more effective when students are older and more aware of the consequences of their actions. Furthermore, some educators and researchers increasingly contend that there is no one best method to teach conflict resolution and that instead, schools and community organizations should utilize a variety of approaches and techniques. Groups also advocate for lifelong conflict resolution training and education. The emergence of new technologies, including the Internet and video games, has provided opportunities for conflict resolution training. For instance, one British study discovered that online mediation programs were 80 percent successful in reducing conflict in the workplace. One result of the renewed attention on preventing violence and abuse has been increased attention on the root causes of conflict and strife and how schools, communities, and families can use education to prevent problems.

In the following chapter, journalists, political scientists, and other researchers explore the methods by which conflict resolution can be taught. The authors explore traditional teaching methods and new strategies, including the use of video games. The viewpoints in this chapter focus on the most effective ways to teach conflict resolution and the most effective methods to prevent youth violence and abuse.

> *"Collaborative training and processes need not and should not stop at the school doors."*

Conflict Resolution Can Be Taught at All Educational Levels

Peter T. Coleman and Beth Fisher-Yoshida

The following viewpoint argues that conflict resolution can be effectively taught throughout life. In fact, for conflict resolution strategies in schools to be effective, the authors contend, adults throughout the community should be familiar with the same tactics and techniques used in the educational system. Peter T. Coleman is the director of the International Center for Cooperation and Conflict Resolution (ICCCR) and an assistant professor of psychology and education at Columbia University. Beth Fisher-Yoshida is the associate director of the ICCCR.

As you read, consider the following questions:

1. What reason do the authors give to support their belief that conflict should not always be viewed as a negative occurrence?

2. What age group was the focus of the Peaceful Kids Early Childhood Social-Emotional Conflict Resolution Program, according to the viewpoint?

3. Are most conflict resolution programs in schools directed toward children or the adults that work in the educational system, according to the authors?

In 2001, 17.3 [percent] of high school students in the United States admitted to carrying a weapon in the past 30 days. Reported incidents of school violence remain at an all-time high, with 1 in 20 students claiming to have missed school during the 30 days preceding the survey because they felt too unsafe to go. Alienated youth between the ages of 15–19 continue to commit suicide at an alarmingly increasing rate. And ongoing conflicts between parents, teachers, administrators, different racial and ethnic groups, and members of vastly disparate socioeconomic groups in schools continue to have destructive consequences on the quality of life and education of young people.

A Culture of Violence

It would be a mistake to assume that the causes of such problems reside only or primarily in the school. Child abuse and neglect, a culture of violence, economic and social injustice, the easy availability of weapons, and many other factors contribute to the occurrence of personal and interpersonal conflict and violence but are largely not under school control. Nevertheless, there is much that schools and communities can do to prevent violence and alienation and counteract the harmful influences emanating from outside the school. In recent years it has been increasingly recognized that schools and communities have to change in basic ways if we are to raise and educate children so they are *for* rather than *against* one another, so they develop the ability to resolve their conflicts constructively rather than destructively, and so they are prepared to contribute to the development of a peaceful and just world.

Our approach focuses on reorienting people from viewing conflict as a negative and destructive occurrence, to seeing the potential, when it exists, for positive change and growth. We target change at the individual, group, societal, and international levels by facilitating a shift in knowledge, attitudes, skills, and social conditions from predominantly competitive and oppressive to fundamentally cooperative and just. Complementary strategies and action research methods are used to engage different elements of the system and to monitor and sustain the effectiveness of such changes.

Conflict resolution concepts and skills can be applied at any stage of our lives and in most situations. The International Center for Cooperation and Conflict Resolution (ICCCR) has had the opportunity to work with different age groups in a variety of settings. In this section, we outline three different projects to illustrate our approach.

The Peaceful Kids Program

The Peaceful Kids Early Childhood Social-Emotional (ECSEL) Conflict Resolution Program and curriculum was created in 1997 to meet the need for a developmentally appropriate, theory-based approach to promoting social/emotional, cognitive, and conflict resolution skills development in preschoolers (aged 2–6). The ICCCR received a 4-year grant from the Hewlett Foundation to develop, test, and disseminate the program in three cities: Boston, Dallas, and Los Angeles. We worked with Head Start staff, parents, and children, focusing on the social-emotional skills underlying constructive conflict resolution. Children were taught to identify their emotions and to use language to express them. A variety of youth-friendly mediums, such as song and dance, were used to teach these skills. Parents and staff were taught the same concepts and skills so they could model and reinforce these behaviors for the children.

From Fall 1997 through Fall 1999, an evaluation of this program occurred in 18 classrooms in day care Head Start centers around the country. Each classroom was randomly assigned to one of three conditions: ECSEL training for (a) day care staff, parents, and children, (b) day care staff and children (but not their parents), and (c) control, no-training. As predicted, children in the condition where both parents and day care staff were trained showed significant increases in assertiveness, cooperation, and self-control, and significant decreases in aggressiveness and socially withdrawn behavior. Parents receiving training showed significant reductions in authoritarian and permissive parenting styles and an increase in authoritative parenting style.

High School Study

The Alternative High School Longitudinal Field Study was our first major project focused on adolescents, and began in the spring of 1988. The objective was to determine the effects of introducing cooperative learning and training in constructive conflict resolution to adolescents undergoing the difficult circumstances typically found in attending an alternative high school in New York City. The results of the 2-year field study showed that the combination of cooperative learning and conflict resolution training resulted in the students demonstrating a marked improvement in their ability to manage their conflicts, which in turn led to their experiencing increased social support and less victimization from others. This improvement in relations with others led to an increase in self-esteem, a decrease in feelings of anxiety and depression, and to more frequent positive feelings of well-being. Higher self-esteem, in turn, produced a greater sense of personal control over their own fates. These changes were also positively associated with higher academic performances.

The following year, ICCCR contracted with the New York City Board of Education and conducted a 2-year project to train one mediation and one negotiation specialist in every high school in New York City. Following this initiative, principals and assistant principals in every New York City high school were also trained in conflict resolution. This initiative included an internal evaluation component conducted by the New York City Board of Education.

The United Nations Study

The United Nations [UN] Consultation and Training Project was started in 1995 to offer training and support in conflict resolution to the leadership and staff of the UN Secretariat. Since that time, we have offered numerous workshops in collaborative negotiation and mediation, as well as cross-cultural training and consultation to all levels of staff and management of the UN, worldwide. Internal consumer satisfaction research on these initiatives has consistently supported their usefulness and popularity. In addition, since 1998 we have co-sponsored and co-taught a course at the UN with the UN Studies Program and the Center for International Conflict Resolution of the Columbia School of International and Public Affairs on "Preventative Diplomacy and Conflict Resolution in the United Nations: Integrating Theory and Practice." Participants in this course engage in lively dialogue with top scholars and practitioners and have included the leadership and staff of UN agencies and diplomatic missions including several UN ambassadors.

The preceding three examples were offered to illustrate how we take conflict resolution concepts and skills and tailor them to the particular audience with whom we are working. These examples also demonstrate our efforts to work across the lifespan, influencing preschoolers, adolescents, educators, and international peacemakers. We operate on the premise that understanding the principles behind cooperative conflict resolution, and learning to develop the skills to apply them, leads to more constructive outcomes for all involved.

Implementation at Multiple Levels

Systemic approaches to intervening in schools and communities reflects the notion that (a) individuals are often members of groups—they affect these groups and are affected by them; (b) groups are components of organizations that affect them and that they affect; and (c) a similar two-way causation exists between the organizations and their communities. It also reflects the understanding that any particular school program, such as conflict resolution training for students, must be seen as one of the many influences in the programs and activities within and outside the school (e.g., cooperative learning, competitive grading, etc.), which may support or counteract the influence of the conflict resolution program.

There are four levels of school systems where one can introduce cooperation and conflict resolution concepts, skills, and processes: the student disciplinary system, the curriculum, the pedagogy (science of teaching), and the school culture. We suggest that adding a fifth level, the community, will enhance the view of the school system as an "open system" embedded in a larger communal system, which can aid in the sustainability of school system change. Interventions at these five levels differ considerably, as outlined below.

Peer Mediation Programs

When there are conflicts that the disputing parties are not able to resolve constructively themselves, it is useful to turn to the help of third parties, such as mediators. To deal with such conflicts, mediation programs have been established in a number of schools. Typically in these programs, both students and teachers are selected and given between 10 and 30 hours of training and follow-up supervision to prepare them to serve as mediators. Students as young as 10 years old, as well as

The Rise in Violence in U.S. Schools Over the Past Ten Years			
School Year	**Number of Reported Violent Incidences**	**Fatalities**	**Wounded**
1997–1998	43	46	73
1998–1999	19	29	41
1999–2000	54	36	85
2000–2001	73	34	70
2001–2002	81	12	137
2002–2003	53	30	46
2003–2004	124	42	118
2004–2005	164	37	215
2005–2006	148	17	215
2006–2007	168	71	233

Statistics compiled by editor.

high school and college students, have been trained. The mediation centers in schools get referrals from deans and teachers as well as students. We place peer mediation programs at Level 1 because they are often what schools are most eager for, and they tend to be the easiest and least expensive to implement. This readiness is sometimes in response to an increase in student disciplinary problems, incidents of violence, or the threat of violence. However, peer mediation programs are usually brought into a school to enhance the overall disciplinary system of a school, not replace it.

Research has shown positive effects on student mediators' self-confidence, self-esteem, assertiveness, and general attitudes toward school. At the school level, mediation programs result in a significant drop in disciplinary referrals, detentions, suspensions, and in more positive perceptions of school climate (i.e., less perceived violence and hurtful behavior among students) by both staff and students. However, it is our assessment that mediation programs alone, although useful, are not sufficient to bring about the shift in education that we suggest is needed to prepare students to live in a peaceful world.

Conflict Resolution Training

Many schools and school districts are bringing conflict resolution concepts and skills into the curriculum, either as a course that stands alone or as a unit within existing programs. These curricula provide lessons and activities for preschoolers through university graduates, and focus on such themes as understanding conflict, communication, dealing with anger, cooperation, affirmation, bias awareness, cultural diversity, conflict resolution, and peacemaking. There are many different programs, and contents vary as a function of the age of the students being trained and their background; however, there are some common elements running through most programs. In effect, most conflict resolution training programs seek to instill the attitudes, knowledge, and skills that are conducive to effective, cooperative problem solving and to discourage the attitudes and habitual responses that give rise to win-lose struggles. From a school system perspective, these trainings establish and reinforce a basic frame of reference and language for collaboration, and orient students to a process and skills that are familiar but underutilized.

Pedagogy

To further enhance the learning of conflict resolution skills from specific units or courses, students can practice these skills in their regular subject areas with two teaching strategies: cooperative learning and constructive controversy.

There are five key elements involved in cooperative learning. The most important is *positive interdependence*. Students must perceive that it is to their advantage if other students learn well and to their disadvantage if others do poorly. In addition, cooperative learning requires *face-to-face interaction* among students where their positive interdependence can be expressed in behavior. It also requires *individual accountability* of each member of the cooperative learning group for mastering the material to be learned and for providing appropriate support and assistance to each other. Further, it is necessary for students to be trained in the *interpersonal and small group skills* needed for effective cooperative work in groups. Finally, cooperative learning also involves providing students with the time and procedures for *processing*, or analyzing, how well their learning groups are functioning and what can be done to improve how they work together. In addition, it is desirable to compose cooperative learning groups so they are heterogeneous with regard to gender, academic ability, ethnic background, and physical disability.

Teachers, no matter what subject they teach, can stimulate and structure constructive controversy in the classroom. This will promote academic learning and development of conflict resolution skills. There are five phases involved in the structured controversy. First, the paired students learn their respective positions; then, each pair presents its position. Next, there is an open discussion where students advocate strongly and persuasively for their positions. After this, there is a perspective-reversal and each pair presents the opposing pair's position as sincerely and as persuasively as they can. In the last phase, students drop their advocacy of their assigned position and seek to reach consensus on a position that is supported by the evidence. In this phase, they write a joint statement with the rationale and supporting evidence for the synthesis their group has agreed on. Constructive controversy has been found to enhance people's understanding of opposing positions and encourage a better integration of diverse ideas, which results in higher quality solutions to problems, more productive work and strengthened relationships.

The School Culture

Most training and intervention concerning cooperation and conflict resolution in schools throughout the United States focuses primarily on children. This focus denies the reality that most adults working in school systems have had little preparation, training, or encouragement to conduct their own work collaboratively or to manage their own conflicts constructively, let alone teach these skills to others. A culture of competition, authoritarianism, coercion, and contention still appears to reign supreme in U.S. schools. For example, research has shown that destructive interpersonal and intergroup conflicts are one of the major obstacles inhibiting the successful implementation of important school initiatives such as site-based management and shared decision making in schools.

In order for school systems to take full advantage of the gains brought by peer mediation programs and conflict resolution curricula, the adults in schools also must receive instruction. This, unfortunately, is often an area of significant resistance. However, adult instruction can be accomplished through two means: individual level work in collaborative negotiation skills, and by working to restructure the school's adult dispute management system. Collaborative negotiation training for adults often parallels the training offered to students, but focuses on problems that are more germane to the personal and professional life of adults. We stress that all adults in schools should be trained (teachers, administrators, counselors, bus drivers, lunch room aids, coaches, etc.). Such extensive training can be expensive, but the costs can be significantly reduced by the training of in-house staff initially, who then become trainers themselves for other school personnel. Such training engenders commitment from the adults. In so doing, it can help to institutionalize the changes through adult modeling of the desired attitudes and behaviors for the students.

University campuses have also begun applying conflict management systems design techniques to campus disputes. The restructuring of a dispute management system encourages movement away from the use of administrative authority and litigation to resolve conflict (power-based and rights-based approaches, respectively) towards a greater emphasis on negotiations and mediations between disputants.

The Broader Community

Collaborative training and processes need not and should not stop at the school doors. In fact, many of the student conflicts originate outside of school—at home, on the school bus, or at social events. Parents, caretakers, clergy, police officers, members of community organizations, and others should be trained in conflict resolution and involved in the overall planning process for preventing destructive conflict among children and youths. We encourage school administrators and conflict resolution practitioners to envision the school system as embedded in a larger community system that, ideally, can be brought into this change process in order to better stabilize school change.

> "*Healthy, socially competent develop-
> ment requires knowledge of negotiation
> and conflict resolution abilities.*"

Conflict Resolution Is Best Taught to Young Children

Anita Vestal and Nancy Aaron Jones

*The following viewpoint details the importance of conflict resolu-
tion training for young children, especially preschoolers. The authors highlight a number of studies that demonstrate the positive
impact that dispute avoidance programs have on children from
lower-income households and how such efforts can reduce violence and conflict in later life. Trained children were far less
likely to resort to violence or confrontation in contentious situations. Anita Vestal teaches at Mountain State University in West
Virginia, and Nancy Aaron Jones directs the Developmental Psy-
chophysiology Laboratory at Florida Atlantic University.*

As you read, consider the following questions:

1. Why is conflict resolution instruction important for
   Head Start families?

2. Name some examples of "negative" negotiation skills.

Anita Vestal and Nancy Aaron Jones, "Peace Building and Conflict Resolution in Preschool Children," *Journal of Research in Childhood Education*, vol. 19, December
2004, p. 131. Copyright © 2004 by the Association for Childhood Education International. Reproduced by permission.

3. According to a study of violence, by what age are violent behaviors resistant to change?

Children learn early in life how to negotiate with one another. Although conflict resolution programs are finding acceptance in grade schools, most programs in early care and education have not yet integrated peace-building strategies into their preschool setting. While a growing body of literature on social and emotional learning points to the advantage of early exposure, empirical assessments of conflict resolution during preschool education are lacking. Moreover, assessments of children who are most at risk for experiencing greater conflict-ridden and violent environments are necessary because these environments have been shown to produce more dysfunctional social skills. One recent study demonstrated that preschool children of middle-income families benefited from conflict resolution training. Thus, a study documenting the effectiveness of teaching conflict resolution skills to preschoolers in low-income and conflict-ridden environments is needed.

Conflict in Human Society

Conflict naturally occurs in human interaction and, if managed properly, can be a very constructive avenue for needed change. Unfortunately, conflict often causes emotional upset and challenges the communication capacity of most adults. Adults and children need to have a set of strategies that will enable them to manage situations and achieve their goals while helping others to achieve their goals as well. Being skilled in social problem solving provides children with a sense of mastery that is needed to cope with stressful life events. Moreover, researchers have linked impaired problem-solving in preschool children with a lack of social skills that undermines peer competence. In addition, possessing skills for solving problems and resolving conflict reduces the risk of adjustment difficulties in children, even children from low-income and troubled families.

Historically, theories and research have suggested that preschoolers would not be able to take the perspective of another within a conflict in order to come to a mutually satisfying outcome. More recent empirical investigations have challenged this view, however, arguing that young children can learn the foundational skills for solving conflicts. Such instruction is particularly important for Head Start families [low-income families in the federally funded preschool program], because these families are likely to experience more conflict. A better understanding of the risks and protective factors affecting Head Start children is essential, considering that young children growing up in poverty are exposed to dramatic increases in the frequency, intensity, and severity of community and family violence. Often, their impoverished neighborhoods are the scenes of violence and crime, leading to a recursive negative cycle of social interaction. Head Start teachers are working with children from the poorest families in America, whose homes are located in unsafe and crime-ridden neighborhoods. The importance of examining the effects of conflict resolution training for Head Start students and the teacher's role in benefiting students is essential, because learning to deal with conflict promotes more socially competent behaviors.

Effects of Children's Exposure to Violence

Researchers who have studied violence and its effects on children consistently have reported that the cycle of violence can become perpetual in areas affected by higher levels of community violence. It is clear that in violent communities, children and their parents begin to accept, and expect, violence. When they are continually exposed to aggression and violence, whether in the neighborhood, at school, in the home, or on television, children begin to model it. When a child feels victimized by his or her environment or feels that the environment instigates aggression, the child is likely to act out aggressively. Exposure to violence increases the risk that children will engage in future violence and other antisocial acts.

Children are more vulnerable to the effects of violent environments when it occurs at an early age. [Scholars] studied distress symptoms that were associated with exposure to violence. They found that exposed children had greater difficulty concentrating in school, memory impairments, anxious attachments with their parents, aggressive play patterns, uncaring behaviors, and self-imposed limitations in their activities, due to fear of violence. These children demonstrated antisocial behaviors as early as the toddler and preschool years. In order to break the cycle of violence, new ways of handling anger and resolving conflict must be introduced early. School age may be too late to introduce conflict resolution skills, especially for children who are exposed to violent environments.

Prosocial skills need to be taught to the very youngest children. One of the critical challenges of educators and communities must be to develop emotional and social competence in our children. The American Psychological Association (APA) has issued several reports that outline remedies to this dilemma; one of the most critical of these remedies is covered in this study—implementing early childhood interventions that are directed toward child care providers (among others) to build the critical foundation of attitudes, knowledge, and behavior to prevent violence. Moreover, [one study] points out that past research clearly demonstrated that school-based intervention can enhance prosocial responding and cooperation, and that preschoolers can learn interpersonal problem-solving skills. Research studies are now needed to identify the elements that are effective within the situational conditions and that are effective for at-risk students so that programs can be implemented expeditiously. . . .

This investigation focused on teaching preschool children about resolving conflicts, endeavoring to determine whether preschool children who are already exposed to violence in their environment have the capacity to learn and use conflict resolution strategies. While not directly instructing the pre-schoolers, it was expected that environment-based changes, via the teacher instruction and the curriculum, would posi-tively affect the preschoolers' conflict resolution skills. During recent years, there has been a rise in the use and evaluation of violence prevention models in schools. However, empirical studies of conflict resolution in preschool are still lacking. Es-tablishing research-based evidence of the significance of con-flict resolution programs in early education has been elusive, perhaps due, in part, to a lack of assessments appropriate for the preschool populations or due to the theory that children lack the intellectual capacities for problem-solving behavior. This study did demonstrate significant gains in preschoolers' ability to resolve interpersonal problems when children were exposed to a conflict resolution curriculum by a teacher trained in socio-emotional skills, conflict resolution skills, and peace education. Specifically, the children were able to report more solutions to a conflict situation, report more relevant compared to irrelevant solutions and, most important, convey fewer forceful (and therefore more prosocial) solutions to conflict situations. This study supports other theories and evi-dence that young children can learn to resolve their conflicts.

Preschoolers

Although preschoolers may lack the higher level of cognitive processing ability necessary to take the perspective of another, and thereby come to a mutually satisfying resolution to con-flict, early learning theories have suggested that children can (and strive to) model behaviors of more competent peers and adults. Within this study, the teachers modeled emotionally competent behaviors to children in the experimental group, and these children used these strategies to resolve conflicts when interviewed by another adult. These results suggest that an environmental change and a curriculum designed to teach adaptive problem-solving principles can effectively teach Head Start children to use and adopt conflict resolution strategies into their understanding of social interactions. Therefore, although young children may be limited by their cognitive maturation, theorists and practitioners should recognize that understanding of conflict and its resolution can occur at different levels of processing. Preschool children are capable of evaluating the consequences of their choices if taught foundational skills. Understanding conflict resolution as a socially competent behavior, with the building blocks based on knowledge of emotions and diversity, may help young children model and adopt good strategies for dealing with conflict in their environment. Ultimately, healthy, socially competent development requires knowledge of negotiation and conflict resolution abilities.

The results of this study also indicate that trained children were better able to come up with non-forceful solutions to a peer conflict than were the children who were not in the trained group. It is essential that children learn prosocial methods for resolving conflict and dealing with hostile emotions as early in life as possible. Researchers recognize the need to diminish the models of aggression in a child's environment and to break the cycle of violence that leads children to model the aggressive approaches they may observe early in life. A key finding was that trained children were able to expand upon problem-solving strategies that significantly reduced the ratio of forceful solutions to interpersonal problems. Conflict resolution training at an early age can help them expand the realm of prosocial responses to choose from when confronted with interpersonal conflicts. The ICPS [I Can Problem Solve] curriculum used in this study contains a set of skills consistent with identified components of peace education models. This study confirms the suitability of an interpersonal cognitive problem-solving model like ICPS for teaching conflict resolution to Head Start and other preschool children between the ages of 3 and 6.

Impact of Conflict Resolution Training

As further evidence of the importance for conflict resolution training, the untrained children in the present study and those before training in [a separate study] used more negative types of negotiation skills (e.g., forcing, withdrawing) as the major strategies for managing conflict. These negative strategies lead to more conflict and violence. Moreover, a more comprehensive study of violence demonstrated that violent behaviors are evident in kindergartners, that they tend to persist and intensify, and that the violent behaviors are resistant to change by early school age. Therefore, violence prevention and intervention should begin as soon as possible.

The choice of a Head Start program as the research site for this study afforded many benefits and opportunities that had not been examined previously. First, teachers (and the Head Start staff who participated in the pilot study) were motivated to learn methods for resolving conflicts that could be taught to the children. Even the control group agreed to participate in the study (instead of taking the college course, they were merely given the ICPS materials after the completion of the study). Second, and on a related note, the participating Head Start centers are located in areas where children and families are most at risk for experiencing conflict-ridden and violent environments. Studies within these environments are necessary because teachers, children, and families are at greater risk for exposure to violent and aggressive behaviors in their daily encounters. Moreover, prior research has established that violent and aggressive environments generate more dysfunctional social skills. Combining the factors of an at-risk environment with the positive motivation of the teachers to adopt a conflict resolution program in the classroom offered an important opportunity to propose and test the theory that teachers should experience a transformation in their own attitudes and beliefs about conflict in order to effectively teach the skills of conflict resolution to children.

Self-Transformation

An important premise in peace education is that self-transformation must occur for lasting empowerment and change to take hold. Building upon the precept of self-transformation, findings demonstrated that teacher transformation in their knowledge, attitudes, and behavior can effect changes in the classroom environment and their teaching methods. The presumed transformation is based specifically on teachers' associations to conflict resolution, violence prevention, and peace education. This effect was demonstrated at least in part by the change in teacher dialogue; that is, after training, teachers used more dialogue that promoted healthy conflict resolution strategies than before the training. Moreover, the researchers attempted to improve teachers' efficiency by imparting the idea that curriculum changes will affect the future abilities of the children in the trained teachers' classrooms. This effect promoted changes in the environment and teaching methods, resulting in a total-student body approach to experiencing conflict resolution strategies.

The two key findings in this study of Head Start teachers and 4- to 5-year-old children are that: 1) preschool children from at-risk neighborhoods can be taught to think of more ways (particularly, more prosocial ways) to resolve interpersonal conflicts than their untrained peers; and 2) when taught by motivated teachers who have undergone transformative training in conflict resolution strategies, preschoolers can acquire significant problem-solving skills. A future study should assess whether these changes in curriculum and childhood cognitive strategies have a lasting effect on children's interactive behaviors across time.

"*A Force More Powerful is designed as the first PC game with nonviolent conflict resolution as its ultimate goal.*"

Video Games and Other Nontraditional Means Are Effective Tools to Teach Conflict Resolution

Reena Jana

In the viewpoint that follows, the journal Business Week Online *offers a review of the video game* A Force More Powerful. *The developers of the game say they sought to integrate nonviolent methods of conflict resolution into something that would be fun to play, but that would also match the "real world." The product was the collaboration of game designers, activists, and documentary filmmakers who sought to create something that would be more effective than older, more traditional training techniques for nonviolent activists.*

As you read, consider the following questions:

1. Upon what countries are the game's fictional scenarios based, according to the viewpoint?

2. According to the author, is *A Force More Powerful* designed mainly as a training tool or an entertainment product?

3. What were some of the strategies that the designers used to increase "enthusiasm" for game players, as stated in the viewpoint?

Imagine a computer-game villain based on a combination of some of history's most brutal dictators—say, Slobodan Milosevic [of Serbia] and Augusto Pinochet [of Chile] rolled into one. *A Force More Powerful*, a strategy game set for February [2005] release, pits players against a character with the traits of such notoriously oppressive and violent rulers. The catch: Gamers can use only brains, not brawn, to overthrow their foes. *A Force More Powerful* is designed as the first PC [personal computer] game with nonviolent conflict resolution as its ultimate goal—and peace marches and labor strikes as the means to get there.

"We didn't set out to reform the game industry or make a statement against violent computer games," says Steve York, the Washington, D.C.–based documentary filmmaker who initiated the project. "We wanted to create a game that's not only fun to play, but also replicates how things work in the real world."

Civil Disobedience and Conflict Resolution

Developed by York's production company, York Zimmerman, and the International Center on Nonviolent Conflict [ICNC], and designed by Hunt Valley, Md.–based Breakaway Games, *A Force More Powerful* consists of 10 fictional scenarios, such as forcing a government to hold free elections, freeing a dissident from prison, or promoting the cause of organized labor. The narratives are based on true grassroots movements in Chile, Denmark, India, the Philippines, Poland, and other countries—including the U.S.

The Object of the Game

The game doesn't require an itchy trigger finger or keen hand-to-eye coordination; rather, it relies entirely on strategy. As well as historical recreations, players can set up their own scenarios, based on their own situation on the ground, and experiment with different nonviolent strategies. The game's artificial intelligence calculates the results.

"You start with just a couple of students under your control, so you plan parties and meetings, working within society to build up the strength of your group," said Break-Away CEO [chief executive officer] Douglas Whatley, outlining one possible game scenario.

Chris Kohler,
"Sir, the Gamers Are Revolving,"
Wired, *October 27, 2005.*

Though devoid of flashy 3D animation a la *Call of Duty*, the game features intricately detailed urban landscapes in which players stage acts of civil disobedience. Players progress by analyzing and selecting fictional characters to join their cause. Then they choose from a list of 84 possible acts of protest to execute.

The game's artificial-intelligence [AI] engine decides whether to arrest, shoot, or ignore the protesters. A player's progress is measured by the number of characters who join or abandon the movement—and whether the oppressive regime is overturned. The game also boasts scenario-editor software that allows customization, such as plugging in elements like scanned maps of real countries or cities, or importing photographs and biographical data of actual people.

Learning by Doing

Although *A Force More Powerful* is primarily intended for real-life activist training, York believes it could find popularity as an innovative strategy game. According to the latest statistics from industry researcher NPD Group, strategy games generated $249 million in revenue in the 12 months prior to November 2005. While this is a dip from the $274 million generated in 2004, the Entertainment Software [Association's] most recent published statistics state that 27% of all PC games sold are strategy titles, representing the largest sales across all categories of PC games. By comparison, shooters make up only 16% of the PC-game market.

A Force More Powerful has its roots in a three-hour PBS documentary series of the same name, produced by York Zimmerman and broadcast in 2000. The film's creative team followed up with a book, published in 2000, and a second documentary on the ousting of Slobodan Milosevic, called *Bringing Down a Dictator*. They also founded the ICNC, which is based in Washington [D.C.].

"The films were never intended to be used for training activists, but audience members informed us they were used that way," says York. "We thought there must be another tool that would be more effective. The best method is learning by doing, and a video game lets people engage in actual conflict or struggle," York adds. So York Zimmerman began developing the game in 2002.

Virtual Tyrants

One challenge was to design a game capable of simulating complex social interaction. "That meant coming up with a game engine based on economic, social, and political factors," York says. He went out and bought turn-based strategy games like *Age of Empires* and *Tropico*, which feature historical battles and drawn-out scenarios, to see how long, slow processes had translated to the computer screen. York Zimmerman then hired Breakaway Games, the company that developed *Tropico*, as well as a number of "serious games," such as emergency-response simulations used by schools and hospitals.

Another challenge was to come up with governmental nemeses that were believable. Having made films about a variety of dictators, York Zimmerman compiled data from its research. "We came up with a pretty comprehensive catalog of dictator behaviors, based on how they impose rules or how they react to opposition against their reigns," York says.

In order to inject the game with a sense of authenticity, York brought on Ivan Marovic—one of the founders of Serbian student movement Optor, which helped to topple Milosevic in the 1990s—as a "design associate." Marovic has been a self-described gamer for 20 years, since he was a 12-year-old with a Commodore 64 [computer game system released in 1982]. He now works as a consultant for pro-democracy groups around the world.

Small Victories

Marovic solved two vital game-design issues. The first was how to bring the aspect of emotion into game play. "I added the ideas of fear and enthusiasm," says Marovic. "I learned from experience that if enthusiasm is low, people are not willing to join a movement."

He adds, "Support doesn't mean much if fear is high. If they think there will be violence, protesters will stay at home. I wanted to bring these ideas into the game."

Marovic suggested that the designers could increase enthusiasm by offering players small victories on the path to the final objective. For example, a player can organize a protest in front of a civic building and recruit more allies, so enthusiasm—measurable by the number of new recruits—goes up. The AI engine playing the role of the oppressive regime usually plays on fear and starts arresting or killing protesters at the next event. Protesters then can retaliate and gain enthusiasm by staging a candlelight vigil for the victims.

"A Real Brain Cracker"

The other game-design problem that Marovic addressed was making sure the AI was believably irrational. "At first, the AI was pretty good and could give you a hard time, but it was more logical than most dictators," he says. "So we added irrational things, like a ruler wasting money even if he is a greedy kleptocrat," says Marovic.

"You don't want dictator AI without traits that are irrational," he says. "Otherwise, the game play is too mechanistic. Now it's a real brain cracker." And Marovic, the gamer and grassroots activist, would know.

> "*Educators have responded to the perceived threat of school violence by implementing programs designed to prevent, deter, and respond to the potential for violence.*"

Schools Employ a Variety of Conflict Resolution Tactics

Susan Jekielek, Brett Brown, Pilar Marin, and Laura Lippman

In the viewpoint that follows, the authors report the results of a study examining the various forms of conflict resolution training used in U.S. schools. The study explores the various tactics implemented at different grade levels—primary through high school—and the differences revealed in urban and rural educational systems. The authors point out that some programs are more popular and more effective than others. Susan Jekielek, Brett Brown, Pilar Marin, and Laura Lippman are researchers at the Child Trends Databank, a research facility in Washington, D.C., that focuses on children and young adults.

Susan Jekielek, Brett Brown, Pilar Marin, and Laura Lippman, "Public School Practices for Violence Prevention and Reduction: 2003–04," *Issue Brief*, National Center for Education Statistics, September 2007. www.eric.ed.gov.

As you read, consider the following questions:

1. What are the most common forms of disciplinary action taken in response to school violence, according to the authors?
2. What does the viewpoint state is the percentage of high schools that monitor activity with security cameras?
3. According to the authors, are urban or rural schools more likely to provide conflict resolution training? Why?

School violence can lead to a disruptive and threatening environment, physical injury, and emotional stress, all of which can be obstacles to student achievement. Educators have responded to the perceived threat of school violence by implementing programs designed to prevent, deter, and respond to the potential for violence in schools. In addition, the No Child Left Behind Act of 2001 emphasizes the importance of safe learning environments by requiring schools to have a safety plan in place and to fund programs and practices intended to prevent and reduce violence in schools.

Violence Education Programs

The needs and capabilities of schools may differ; thus, schools implement a variety of practices intended to prevent and reduce violence. However, little is known about the prevalence of school practices and the extent to which they vary according to school characteristics. This Issue Brief (1) examines principals' reports of the prevalence of formal practices in public schools designed to prevent or reduce school violence and (2) describes the distribution of these practices by selected school characteristics.

This analysis is based on school-level data reported by principals participating in the school year 2003–04 School Survey on Crime and Safety (SSOCS), administered by the U.S. Department of Education's National Center for Education Statistics (NCES). The estimates presented here comple-

The Decline of Overall School Violence

Extremely violent events in schools draw our attention to programs designed to prevent and reduce school violence. Highly publicized school shootings, though tragic, are thankfully rare. In fact, less than 1 percent of the over 2,000 homicides of school-aged children in the 1999–2000 school year happened at school. Further, over the past 10 years, victimization of school-aged children has declined both at and away from school. Nevertheless, some forms of antisocial behavior are common in schools. For example, according to principal reports from the 1999–2000 school year, 71 percent of public schools experienced a violent crime and over half took serious disciplinary action for some children.

Sandra Jo Wilson and Mark W. Lipsey,
The Effectiveness of School-Based Violence Prevention
Programs for Reducing Disruptive and Aggressive Behavior,
September 2005. www.ncjrs.gov.

ment those in the NCES report *Indicators of School Crime and Safety: 2006,* which reported on the safety and security measures taken by schools in school year 2003–04. In addition to including updated estimates, this analysis reports on additional safety and security practices, such as the use of security officers at public schools, and a variety of other approaches intended to prevent and reduce school violence.

There are many approaches designed to prevent and reduce violence in schools. However, this study examines (1) efforts to involve parents in preventing and reducing violence, (2) safety and security procedures and (3) allowable disciplinary policies. In addition to reporting the data by standard school characteristics, the study presents results by principals' self-reports of community crime.

Prevalence of Violence and Conflict Resolution

Among efforts to involve parents, 59 percent of schools formally obtained parental input on policies related to school crime and 50 percent provided parental training to deal with students' problem behaviors. In addition, 21 percent of schools involved parents at school to maintain discipline.

For each of the following safety and security procedures examined, less than half of the schools used any one of the six procedures. Forty-five percent of schools had security officers or police present on a regular basis, 36 percent used one or more security cameras to monitor the school, 21 percent used dogs to conduct random drug checks, 14 percent required students to wear uniforms, 13 percent conducted random sweeps for contraband, and 6 percent performed random metal detector tests on students.

In terms of the three disciplinary policies examined, 68 percent of schools allowed out-of-school suspension with no curriculum or services provided, 67 percent allowed transfer to a specialized school for disciplinary reasons, and 51 percent allowed removal from school for at least the remainder of the year with no services.

Differences by School

Primary schools were more likely than high schools to provide training for parents to deal with students' problem behaviors (55 vs. 38 percent) or involve parents at school to maintain school discipline (24 vs. 17 percent).

Four of the six safety and security measures were more common in high schools than in middle and primary schools. For example, a greater percentage of high schools than middle and primary schools used one or more security cameras to monitor the school (60 percent vs. 42 and 28 percent, respectively). In addition, a greater percentage of high schools than middle and primary schools had security officers or police present on a regular basis (72 percent vs. 64 and 34 percent, respectively).

Differences were also found in allowable disciplinary policies by school level. For example, 85 percent of high schools allowed out-of-school suspensions, compared with 77 percent of middle schools and 60 percent of primary schools. Furthermore, a greater percentage of high schools than middle and primary schools allowed removal of a student from school for at least the remainder of the year (70 percent vs. 59 and 42 percent, respectively).

A smaller percentage of rural schools than city schools provided training to help parents deal with students' problem behaviors (43 vs. 60 percent) or involve parents at school to maintain school discipline (17 vs. 31 percent). Schools in cities and urban fringe areas were more likely than rural schools to require students to wear uniforms (29 and 12 percent, respectively, vs. 5 percent). A greater percentage of city schools than rural schools performed random metal detector checks (12 vs. 3 percent) or had security officers or police present on a regular basis (51 vs. 38 percent). However, rural and town schools were more likely than city and urban fringe schools to use dogs to conduct random drug checks (31 and 32 percent vs. 11 and 16 percent, respectively).

Sixty-one percent of schools with students from high-crime areas had security officers or police present on a regular basis, compared to 39 percent of schools with students from low-crime areas. Schools with students from high-crime areas reported higher levels of all selected safety and security measures than schools with students from low-crime areas, with the exception of using dogs to conduct random drug checks.

Schools with 50 percent or more minority enrollment were more likely to involve parents at school to maintain school discipline than were schools with lower percentages of minority enrollment (30 vs. 13, 16, and 22 percent). Furthermore, 67 percent of schools with 50 percent or more minority enrollment made efforts to formally obtain parental input on policies related to school crime, compared to 57 percent of schools with 5 to 20 percent minority enrollment and 47 percent of schools with less than 5 percent minority enrollment. About one-third of schools (35 percent) with 50 percent or more minority enrollment required students to wear uniforms, compared to 10 percent or less of schools with smaller percentages of minority enrollment. Fifty-two percent of schools with 50 percent or more minority enrollment had security officers or police present on a regular basis, compared to 39 percent of schools with less than 5 percent minority enrollment.

Practices and Results Vary

This Issue Brief found that schools implemented a variety of school violence prevention and reduction practices and that some practices were more commonly used than others. In addition, practices differed by school level and other selected school characteristics. For example, high schools were more likely than primary schools to implement safety and security procedures, while primary schools were more likely than high schools to promote training for parents to deal with students' problem behavior. Also, schools in rural areas showed different patterns of practices than those in urban areas, with rural schools more likely to use dogs for random drug checks and less likely to use other practices—such as student uniforms, involving parents at school to maintain discipline, and random metal detector checks.

"Well-managed conflict can bring wonderful benefits."

Conflicts Usually Result from Divergent Goals

Sarah Gibbard Cook

The following viewpoint, taken from an article published in the journal Women in Higher Education, *explores the causes of interpersonal conflicts among educators on college campuses. The strategies for managing such conflicts are described in a speech given by psychologist and professor Sandra I. Cheldelin, as reported in the journal. Cheldelin explains why such conflicts happen and how they can escalate from minor disagreements into major destructive interactions. For example, a person's individual style of conflict management learned as a child influences how he or she deals with disagreements and divergent goals.* Women in Higher Education *is a news journal geared toward female educators at colleges and universities.*

As you read, consider the following questions:

1. What are the five causes of conflict, according to the viewpoint?

Sarah Gibbard Cook, "Strategies to Manage Conflicts on Campus," *Women in Higher Education*, vol. 16, January 2007, pp. 36–37. Copyright © 2007 Women in Higher Education. All rights reserved. Reproduced by permission.

2. What are the six steps of conflict escalation, as identified by Cheldelin in the viewpoint?

3. According to the viewpoint, what are the five methods of conflict avoidance?

If your campus is free of conflicts, you're either in a honeymoon phase or in denial, or maybe your school is set in its ways and big on avoidance. Where smart, creative, self-assured people are gathered together, clashes of perspective are bound to surface.

Conflict can do harm or good, depending on how it's handled. Keynoting the Wisconsin Women in Higher Education Leadership (WWHEL) conference in Madison [Wisconsin] in October [2006] was **Dr. Sandra Cheldelin**, professor of conflict resolution at the Institute for Conflict Analysis and Resolution at George Mason University [Virginia].

She's a licensed psychologist, experienced mediator and co-author of *Conflict Resolution* and *Conflict: From Analysis to Intervention*. She was provost—not a job for the conflict-averse—at Antioch University [Ohio] before joining George Mason in 1996.

Conflict Sources

Conflict comes from Latin for "striking together with force." Sparks fly when words, emotions and actions strike together. [In her speech, Cheldelin] defined conflict as an expressed struggle between interdependent people or groups who perceive incompatible goals, scarce resources or interference in achieving their goals. "If it's just a misperception, it's easy to resolve with just a touch of good will," she said. When the differences are real, relationships can get dicey.

Many groups have experienced the destructive effects of poorly handled conflict. It undermines good feelings and co-operation, divides the group into factions and deepens differences by legitimizing lack of support for the group.

It discourages honest and open participation; why stick your neck out to get bashed? Turning personal, it diverts attention from the real issues.

Did you ever wake up in the middle of the night thinking, *I can't believe I said that?* "A destructive conflict will end up with behavior you regret," she said.

[Cheldelin] . . . got into a conflict on co-authorship: Which name should be listed first? She won the first round but [her coauthor's] name appeared first on the second edition. Though she knew better, she sent him a nasty email; "I did it with great joy." He wrote back that he had nothing to do with the change.

In contrast, well-managed conflict can bring wonderful benefits. It encourages open discussion and a full exploration of what's on everyone's mind. It gives otherwise-powerless new people a voice and lets new ideas surface.

Communications become authentic and pent-up emotions find release. Diverse individuals build skills and confidence, and the group develops trust in its ability to weather change. The solution to the immediate conflict will be something everyone can live with.

Why Conflicts Happen

Not every difference of opinion is a conflict. You can listen to your favorite music and your friend can listen to hers; but you can't play them both full blast in the same room at the same time, or each take home the same CD if there's only one and you live apart. Conflict occurs when people either want different things and have to settle for the same thing, or want the same thing and have to settle for different things.

Across-the-board budget cuts [in higher education] set departments and faculty scrambling for scarce resources. Curriculum decisions can't offer all things to all people. Threatening, contentious patterns of influence escalate matters, as may personal characteristics such as race or gender.

In *The Mediation Process,* Christopher Moore outlined five causes of conflict [which Cheldelin discussed]:

- *Data disputes.* People have different information or interpret it differently. "These are shockingly common in higher education," Cheldelin said [in her speech].

- *Relationship conflicts.* Bias, stereotypes, poor communication, strong emotions and repeated negative behavior cause interpersonal tensions.

- *Interest conflicts.* When there's only so much money for computers, who gets one? The senior administrators need one to plan a budget, staff need one to track the budget and faculty and students are all supposed to write on a computer.

- *Value conflicts.* Different ways of life or beliefs lead to different criteria for judging behavior. New arrivals don't see things the same as the old guard.

- *Structural conflicts.* Unequal power, authority or distribution of resources is a common source of tension. Campus hierarchy and the tenure system are a set-up for conflict.

Physical structure was an issue where [Cheldelin] worked. Faculty offices were upstairs, not accessible to everyone. Some wanted to pay $180,000 for an elevator. Instead, they eventually moved to a new site where stairs weren't an issue, which changed the whole culture.

The "Other" in Conflicts

"When you create a story about a conflict, you position yourself and the other," she said. You set yourself up as right and the other as wrong (or old, or female or black).

Rom Harré of Georgetown University [in Washington] DC developed positioning theory to describe a more flexible set of relationships than the traditional, static notion of "role." Positions don't have to be forever.

When she first went to the Institute, [Cheldelin recalls that] everyone went straight to their offices without saying hello. She felt unwelcome, positioned as an unwanted outsider. She would go home and cry. Someone asked her, "What are you going to do about it?" So she set about to reposition herself. She stopped by one colleague after another and said "Good morning" until they replied. In effect she was saying, "Hey, I'm here, you could at least say good morning."

"Focus on the story line, not the person," she said [in her speech]. Avoid describing people in metaphors, which position them as unacceptable others:

"She attacked me; she was indefensible."

"He comes in like a hurricane."

"He's stubborn as a mule."

You've stopped talking person-to-person when you see the other as a bomb squad, a storm or an animal. Emotions are bound to rise. Take a break and try again tomorrow, going back to the beginning to undo the negative story line.

How Conflicts Escalate

Conflicts turn ugly by a predictable process:

1. *Attributions.* Here's what I see you doing and what I'm convinced you mean by it.

2. *Commitment.* It's my way or the highway.

3. *Entrapment.* As the problem absorbs more and more time, energy and resources, people dig in and become entrenched in their positions.

4. *Arousal.* The word *sarcasm* comes from Greek for "to tear flesh." Aggression takes the form of hostility, scapegoating and flesh-tearing humor.

5. *Reciprocity.* What goes around comes around. You harmed me so I'll get even.

Conflict and Goals

Conflict exists when one person believes another is interfering with his/her goals.

[Family mediators and conflict managers] Joyce Wilmot and William Hocker believe we have four basic types of goals:

- **Content**—measurable things like money, or the office with the window, or who gets to choose the movie tonight.

- **Process**—how decisions are made.

- **Identity**—or "face," that is, my self-image and social standing.

- **Relational**—how we interact with each other; who leads, follows, shares, cares.

And they suggest that while most conflicts are expressed initially as content or process goals (as in, "I'm sick of working with an ancient computer" or "Who decided this without asking me?"), they are most often about identity and relationships.

Jill Geisler,
"What Kind of Conflict Manager Are You?"
Poynter Online, January 20, 2004.
www.poynter.org/column.asp?id=34&aid=58778.

---

6. *Coalitions.* Opponents line up supporting teams; anyone who isn't with me is against me. This can happen quickly or simmer.

"Faculty who are really smart can do very well at making life a living hell," [Cheldelin] said. She was the only tenure-track woman in a department with a well-established bully. She shut down when he bullied and so did her chair. At the coalition stage, she had the students and women faculty on her side while he had the old-time males.

She finally went to his office one morning and they worked out their differences, to the relief of all of their colleagues. The sooner a conflict can be worked through, the less chance it has to escalate. Initiating collaborative talks with the enemy doesn't come easily for many of us, but sometimes it's necessary.

Personal Styles of Conflict Management

Think of a conflict that's touched you in the last three months. How did you respond? Did you open a discussion, make nice to diffuse the anger or ignore it in the hope it would go away?

We learn styles for handling conflict in our family of origin. [Cheldelin recalls that] when her mother was mad, all the doors got slammed. Her father told her to be nice to everybody, no matter what. Did your family fight openly, slam doors or keep silent? Were you punished if you raised your voice? Was a controversy the elephant in the room that nobody mentioned, or did your family love the drama of a fight? "We learn early on how to cope, based on pecking order. We bring all this stuff to the academy," she said.

Styles for handling conflict fall into five basic categories. You can graph them, with "meeting my needs" on one axis and "meeting others' needs" on the other. Most of us lean toward one or another of these behaviors:

- *Avoiding.* "Leave well enough alone" falls in the corner of the graph that's low on meeting any needs at all.

- *Competing.* "Might makes right" cares about only self.

- *Accommodating.* "Kill the enemy with kindness" falls at the opposite extreme, setting aside one's own needs to meet the needs of others.

- *Compromise.* "Split the difference" sits right in the middle of the graph, meeting some needs of each and leaving other needs unmet.

- *Collaboration.* "Two heads are better than one." At the opposite corner from avoidance, collaboration assigns high value to the needs of everybody involved. It means working together toward a win-win solution.

Conflicts are very situational, and each style has its place. The challenge is to know when and how to intervene.

Strategies for Managing Conflicts

Many conflicts are resolved privately and informally by people with no training in mediation. Do you know the informal peacemakers on your campus? Often they're women. "We're good at it. We do it all the time," she said.

When that doesn't happen, a conflict can take on a life of its own. Cultures, personalities and interests collide. The further it goes, the harder the solution.

Methods of resolving conflicts progress up a scale from informal discussion to lawsuits:

1. Negotiation
2. Facilitation
3. Third-party mediation
4. Non-binding arbitration
5. Binding arbitration
6. Adjudication [lawsuits]

As the scale progresses it gets more formal and confrontational, with winners and losers. Your goal in conflict management is to intercede in the early, less formal stages to reach a consensual solution. Other ideas:

Anticipate potential conflicts. With age comes wisdom of seeing problems before they arise. We learn who never gets along and what's likely to push whose buttons. "Past performance predicts future performances," she said.

Provide a process to deal with conflicts. At the end of a meeting, ask what worked and what didn't. Consider rotating who leads meetings; payback time faces the heavy-handed meeting chair. Depending on the issues, counselors, human resources or ombudswomen can help.

Acknowledge conflicts when they arise. Escalation makes conflicts harder to resolve. She could have been spared a lot of bullying if she'd gone into the bully's office sooner.

Apply a problem-solving model. Define the issues, gather relevant information, generate and evaluate options and select one together. Appreciative inquiry—asking what worked well—raises positive energy for finding shared solutions.

Keep cool. Calm yourself by running, doing yoga and using anger management techniques. Disengage when emotions run high; if it doesn't need to be done right now, take time out.

Use effective communication skills. Listen, rephrase and reframe. Checking your understanding helps you get it right and is a gesture of good faith.

Consider using third parties. If emotions are getting in the way, a neutral party can facilitate communications.

I *"Conflict is necessary for change."*

Conflicts Usually Result from Change

Chuck Kormanski

In the viewpoint that follows, Chuck Kormanski explores the role of change in initiating conflicts. The author argues that change is often the cause of conflict, but it is also usually the result of conflict within groups. Consequently, change can be healthy and useful for groups or organizations, but conflicts must be carefully managed in order to gain these benefits. Kormanski states that the key to beneficial conflict resolution is leadership. Chuck Kormanski is a consultant who teaches at the University of Pittsburgh in Pennsylvania and is the author of The Team: Explorations in Group Process.

As you read, consider the following questions:

1. What does the viewpoint suggest are the nine points for creating both stability and instability?
2. What are the three classifications of conflict identified in the viewpoint?
3. What seven assumptions does the viewpoint assert are necessary for managing change?

Chuck Kormanski, "Change and Conflict in Group Development," *Counseling & Human Development*, vol. 37, March 2005, p.1. Copyright © 2005 Love Publishing Company. Reproduced by permission.

Conflict ... is a naturally occurring behavior pattern and an essential stage in the growth and development of the group. Thus, it is a positive phenomenon and a prerequisite for group growth. Just as algebra and trigonometry are prerequisite for calculus, healthy conflict is necessary for promoting group development.

The Nature of Conflict

Individual development follows a similar pattern. One grows and matures more quickly during periods of personal conflict. A change in schools, a move to a new neighborhood, the loss of a good friend, a family divorce or separation, a change in job status, or the death of someone close—each, in its own unique way, challenges the individual to react in a more responsible manner, to take charge of the situation, to keep control of his or her emotions, to act in an initiatory and decisive way. Conflict frequently brings out the best in each of us as long as we are developmentally ready for the challenge.

The key ... is to manage conflict, not eliminate it. Unmanaged conflict becomes chaos that will create a barrier to the further development of the group. The absence of conflict encourages apathy, which may be worse than chaos because it results in a lack of energy with which to work. Effective leaders are adept at introducing conflict into apathetic groups to increase the energy for change and at reframing chaotic groups to create a focused direction that all members can follow.

Group conflict can result in a number of costs that take a toll on both the people and the finances of today's organizations. The costs include wasted management time, reduced decision quality, loss of skilled employees, restructuring, employee sabotage, lowered motivation, lost work time, and health costs. Indeed, current trends in business and industry may be increasing the level of these costs. The increasing diversity of the workforce is bringing more value, attitude, and behavioral differences into the workplace. Participative management is giving more individuals supervisory responsibilities. With these changes, conflict is increasing.

Conflict and Change

Yet conflict is necessary for change. The use of teams and task forces is providing a natural setting for the group development process to unfold. With this process comes the . . . potential for continued growth.

Trends in educational institutions follow those in business and industry. The challenge of developing a more skillful and adaptable workforce rests on the abilities of our schools to graduate students with the ability to learn. The skills needed in the global marketplace mostly involve communications, computers, and interpersonal relations, including skills in conflict management. We are in the age of information, and creating learning organizations is fast becoming the preferred survival strategy.

[Scholar T.J.] Peters encouraged thriving on chaos and noted that the core paradox that leaders at all levels must face is the need to foster internal stability in order to encourage change. He stressed a view of leadership that establishes direction by developing an inspiring vision, managing by example, and practicing visible management; that empowers people by increased listening, deferring to the front line, delegating, reducing bureaucracy, and increasing horizontal management; and that embraces the process of change. In essence, success will come to those who thrive on chaos and learn how to manage conflict effectively.

Peters posited nine tips for simultaneously creating stability and instability:

- Be out and about (management by walking around).

- Demand empiricism (have everybody evaluate everything).

- Listen (institute listening forums and encourage sharing).

- Laud failure (test fast, fail fast, adjust fast).

- Proclaim speedy horizontal action taking (involve multiple functions).

- Define common denominators (make successful group efforts visible).

- Let customers teach (learn from those you serve).

- Make the workplace fun (take pleasure in successes and failure alike).

- Promote those who deal best with paradox (reward change).

In addition, he suggested that leaders organize as much as possible around teams and that the self-managing team should become the basic organizational building block. Understanding group development theory is critical for putting these ideas into practice. . . .

The Causes of Conflict

As a group gets oriented and dependency upon the leader decreases, an atmosphere of counterdependency begins to surface. Conflict will not always be loud and obvious with illogical ideas and irrational emotions taking center stage. Frequently, it will present itself as differences of opinions, as members presenting a variety of alternatives or choices, or as members suggesting different opportunities for taking action. All of these offer positive possibilities. Sometimes conflict will be subtle, quiet, and hardly noticeable. Identifying conflict of this type involves observing nonverbal behavior, communication patterns, and unmet human needs. If left unattended, such conflict will smolder and eventually create feelings of resentment and a behavior pattern best described as "good old-fashioned" stubbornness.

Change as Part of Life

Everything around us is changing: the seasons change, people change, technology changes, politicians change, laws change. We live in a world of constant change. Changes like moving house, changing friends or changing jobs can be very difficult. However, working with our negative attitudes, anger, hurt and bitterness, or dedicating effort to make internal changes which can produce needed external transformation can be much harder and seem to go on and on.

Changing behavioural patters is never easy and is generally a painful, slow process: taking even years if the changes are major ones.

Kathryn Moura, "The Process of Change," Teaching for Change.

Conflicts may be classified as involving behaviors, attitudes, or values. Behavioral conflicts have been described as approach-approach, avoidance-avoidance or approach-avoidance in reference to a specific goal. The approach-approach conflict involves two or more positive goals. Only one of the goals is attainable at a given point in time, as movement toward it is movement away from the other goal(s). The choice of a college major, a marriage partner, a vacation site, or a movie involves this type of conflict.

The avoidance-avoidance conflict represents the opposite dilemma. One must choose among a number of negative outcomes. Taking the lesser of two evils is the end result. The prospective employee who has to choose an entry-level job from among several in the company when he or she really wants a higher level position and the teenager who must choose among several punishment options for staying out too late are faced with this type of conflict.

Current Check-Outs summary for COLLELLA,
Tue Apr 05 14:07:07 EDT 2011

BARCODE: 31000000659592
TITLE: Conflict resolution opposing vie
DUE DATE: Apr 26 2011

Current Check-Outs summary for COLLELLA,
        Tue Apr 05 14:07:07 EDT 2011

BARCODE: 31000000659592
TITLE: Conflict resolution: opposing vie
DUE DATE: Apr 26 2011

The approach-avoidance conflict occurs when choices contain both positive and negative components. The single approach-avoidance conflict involves deciding whether to approach a goal with a positive-negative mixture; the double approach-avoidance conflict involves more than one mixture choice. Deciding whether to eat at one's first choice of restaurants when it will be necessary to stand in line for an hour is an example of the former, deciding on a job offer or college to attend is an example of the latter.

Attitude and Value Conflicts

Attitude conflicts occur between individuals with different personalities and may involve the way in which events are perceived and are evaluated. Such differences lead to misinterpretations, which may result in defensiveness, misunderstanding, or feelings of being rejected, devalued, or stereotyped. These added complications increase the complexity of the situation and heighten the emotional climate within which the conflict occurs. Issues of control and influence are frequently central to personality conflicts.

Value conflicts are more deeply rooted than other types of conflicts and often come to light in decisions about lifestyle and work style. Our values are not altered as easily or as quickly as are our attitudes or behaviors. In fact, core values that are formed in childhood are quite resistant to change and persist into our adult life. Making a choice between a value that has a negative connotation and one with a positive connotation is relatively easy. Being honest versus dishonest, acting lazy versus being ambitious, and feeling sincere versus feeling insincere are typical examples. Selecting among a number of positive values in a given situation is much more difficult. Should one choose honesty, ambitiousness, or sincerity? We have already chosen most of our values by the time we leave childhood. The real challenge is in prioritizing our values and in dealing with the conflict that comes when we interact with other individuals who hold similar values to ours but have prioritized them in a different manner. In addition, changing situations can create changes in the prioritization of a value set.

Conflict and Leadership

Conflict and leadership are inseparable. As conflict increases, the need for effective leadership increases. Effective leadership within conflict situations mandates both knowledge of and skill in conflict management techniques. The group leader should acknowledge conflict and share the positive benefits that can be derived from it.

Much of leadership involves influencing and controlling change. As our environment becomes more complex and involves increased interpersonal interactions, individual effort has less impact. Group effort is fast becoming the preferred strategy for managing change and teamwork the preferred process. Both rely heavily on group development theory as a basis upon which to build implementation efforts. Education can learn from business and vice versa. Seeing similar problems in a different setting will often provide the necessary perspective for developing innovative solutions.

[Herman] Ohme offered a law of institutional change that suggests that it is not the merit of the plan but the right combination of leadership and member involvement that determines successful outcomes. Such a working relationship is best accomplished through participative management, but only after group members have had some appropriate experience and training. When an organization is willing to make the investment necessary to provide these opportunities to their employees, a new atmosphere surrounding the workplace is possible. As stated by Rosebeth Moss Kanter, "After years of telling corporate citizens to trust the system, many organizations must relearn instead to trust their people".

[There are] seven methodological assumptions for effectively managing change within an organization:

- Starting at points of readiness

- Using a bottom-up, top-down approach

- Making creative use of bureaucracy

- Viewing crisis as opportunity

- Having a clear image of ideal change

- Espousing the attitude of doing things better, not perfectly

- Having a "we can muddle through" philosophy

Strategies that have proven useful as interventions include

- using ad hoc task forces,

- mixing mandated change with creative input,

- using crisis to further change,

- scanning the system for small trouble spots,

- maintaining a holistic policy,

- conceptualizing major efforts as projects, and

- involving everyone in the change process.

People resist change only when it is imposed. Highly involving those who are most affected by the change in the planning process reduces resistance and improves the implementation of the plan. Commitment and ownership are powerful sources of motivation. Ownership in team projects demands a high level of maturity from everyone involved.

Periodical Bibliography

The following articles have been selected to supplement the diverse views presented in this chapter.

Jennifer Batton — "Considering Conflict Resolution Education: Next Steps for Institutionalization," *Conflict Resolution Quarterly*, Fall/Winter 2004.

Karen Levin Coburn and Madge Lawrence Treeger — "12 Steps to Independence," *Newsweek*, May 22, 2006.

Roberta Anna Heydenberk and Warren R. Heydenberk — "The Conflict Resolution Connection: Increasing School Attachment in Cooperative Classroom Communities," *Reclaiming Children and Youth*, September 22, 2007.

Abigail Johnson — "Community Programs Encourage Juvenile Mediation: Parents, Kids Learn to Communicate," *The Indiana Lawyer*, November 5, 2003.

Michael Kelley — "Peace Building and Conflict Resolution in Preschool Children," *Childhood Education*, March 22, 2005.

Reva Klein — "You Can Rebuild It: Dealing with Conflict," *Times Educational Supplement*, August 4, 2006.

Laura Koss-Feder — "Patching It Up," *Time*, January 20, 2003.

Teresa Russell — "Dispute Mediation: The Wisdom of Solomon?" *Human Resources*, May 2, 2006.

Aletha Solter — "Keeping the Peace: Family Meetings for Conflict Resolution," *Mothering*, May–June 2003.

Thomas J. Stickrath and Sarah Wallis — "Reducing Aggression in Juvenile Facilities: Ohio's Plan," *Corrections Today*, June 1, 2007.

Corinna J. Tucker, Susan M. McHale, and Ann C. Crouter — "Conflict Resolution: Links with Adolescents' Family Relationships and Individual Well-Being," *Journal of Family Issues*, September 1, 2003.

OPPOSING
VIEWPOINTS®
SERIES

CHAPTER 2

Is Conflict Resolution a Good Alternative to Legal Action?

Chapter Preface

The legal system in the United States has grown increasingly complex and burdensome for many Americans. Government agencies, schools, businesses, and individuals are confronted with rising costs associated with the spread of lawsuits and other legal actions. A critic of the U.S. legal system, Greg Hickman says, "It has been estimated that American businesses, consumers and governments spend upwards of $80 billion annually on litigation and liability insurance premiums." Meanwhile, many courts have a difficult time keeping pace with the rising tide of litigation. The result is a backlog of cases and lengthy waits for trial. For instance, in 2007 the Texas Supreme Court had 111 cases in which no ruling had been issued during the year even though the trials had occurred, thirty-six others that had waited for more than a year without being tried, and thirteen cases that were more than two years old awaiting trial. Many proponents of alternative dispute resolution techniques claim that these strategies offer a viable alternative to the traditional legal system.

In fact, many states have already embraced legal conflict resolution methods as a way to reduce the number of court cases each year. Instead of going to trial, individuals, companies, and groups can plead their case before a neutral mediator who then renders a binding decision. This method saves time and money, but some argue that it can deprive people of their legal rights and that it offers unfair advantages to one side or another. For instance, some lawyers and other legal professionals worry that mediators may not understand the law or have the same training as those in the legal profession. However, alternative dispute resolution for legal matters has grown increasingly popular around the world. Countries ranging from South Africa to Uruguay to Sri Lanka have successfully implemented alternative judicial systems with substantial savings in money and time. Their success has in turn led more state and local governments in the United States to embrace alternative dispute resolution.

In the subsequent viewpoints, scholars and lawyers examine the implications surrounding the spread of alternative dispute resolution programs as an option other than traditional legal action. The benefits and risks of the conflict resolution techniques are explored. They further examine if the programs save money and effort by analyzing whether or not conflict resolution is a good alternative to lawsuits and court action.

"*The mediator considers a successful outcome one in which everyone is satisfied.*"

Conflict Resolution Is a Practical Way to Avoid Lawsuits

Dick Dahl

In the viewpoint that follows, writer Dick Dahl explores the differences between mediators and litigators, or lawyers, in the context of conflict resolution as set forth in a book by California mediator Jeffrey Krivis. Although both mediators and litigators share many of the same techniques, Krivis states, the two groups often use their skills in different ways. Krivis argues that if lawyers apply similar approaches to those used by mediators, they will be better able to avoid deadlocks in negotiations and reduce the number of cases that go to trial. Dick Dahl is a journalist who writes about legal issues for a variety of U.S. newspapers.

As you read, consider the following questions:

1. How does a litigator define success, according to the viewpoint?

2. What are the main advantages that Krivis asserts lawyers could gain from using mediation tactics?

3. What type of musician does Krivis compare with successful mediators, and why?

L itigators and mediators are not exactly birds of a feather. Although both deal with conflict resolution, they have radically different notions about what constitutes a successful outcome and how to go about achieving it. The litigator defines success as total victory for his client—often at the expense of the opposing party. The mediator considers a successful outcome one in which everyone is satisfied. So what can the trial lawyer learn from the mediator? A lot, says Jeffrey Krivis, a mediator in Encino, California. His new book— *Improvisational Negotiation: A Mediator's Stories of Conflict About Love, Money, Anger—and the Strategies that Resolved Them*—describes a variety of negotiation techniques for breaking up logjams in disputes.

Mediators Versus Litigators

Using actual cases from his 17-year mediation career, Krivis discusses how understanding the emotions and hidden goals behind a dispute can help parties reach a solution they are both satisfied with. Not only can these skills help lawyers prepare for trial and settlement negotiations, they can also improve their day-to-day client relations. "We lawyers are trained to be judgmental," said Krivis. "It's important to be judgmental, but if you let that get in the way of understanding and listening, you miss out on certain key information that helps you move a case forward." Krivis believes that trial lawyers have already developed some of these listening skills from watching closely for jurors' body language and other cues that might help guide their arguments. He said the key in negotiation is to "listen for the unstated." "Some of these listening techniques come from neurolinguistic programming. You're looking for audio, visual and kinesthetic (emotional) signs," he said, referring to the way different people prefer to receive and process information. "Is this person somebody who responds to their emotions? Or do they respond better by hearing something or seeing something? When you start noticing these things, you're able to manage that negotiation through responding to their sensitivity signs." Krivis says the clues can be in a person's speech—"I hear what you're saying," or "I see where you're coming from," or "That doesn't feel right to me." Looking deeper Krivis' book is filled with stories from his own experience as a mediator over the last 17 years, presented to provide lessons for practicing lawyers.

One case study involves a telecommunications employee who sued his employer after he was laid off. The man had worked for the company for 20 years, and took the termination particularly hard. Krivis said the company prepared for the mediation as though they were going to trial, creating PowerPoints and assembling data. But in talking to the former employee, Krivis determined that the man would not respond to legal arguments because the issue was an emotional one for him. When Krivis talked with the man in more detail, he learned that he had lost his parents as a boy. In recent years, he had spent every Thanksgiving with his co-workers, so the company had become like a family to him. To this man, being fired was much more than losing a job—he was losing his family. Krivis explained that to the employer, who then changed course and talked to the man about maintaining a connection to the company. The result was a two-year consultancy deal that satisfied both sides. The lesson here, according to Krivis, is that it's essential to allow people to tell their story. Not only does this help release the emotional intensity that can stand in the way of negotiations, it also gives you a better understanding of what motivates the other side.

Advantages for Lawyers

While lawyers might benefit from these techniques in preparation for trial, Krivis thinks they also can gain an advantage from them in more everyday matters. "Virtually everything is a negotiation. In situations with clients, there's always that tension between 'What am I going to give?' and 'What am I going to take?' This is true whether it involves a retainer agreement, when you're going to meet with the client, or how much work you're going to do." Lawyers are all too familiar with stone faces they periodically encounter when dealing with people. These people are closed, angry, have little affect and seem determined to maintain a hard-line stance. The key to dealing with them, according to Krivis, is to identify what is causing their immovable stance. He said that a stone face is a signal of some sort of strategic or emotional impediment—or both. "When I say strategic, I'm talking about information that people have or that they're concealing because they're looking for a better deal and they think that if they don't show you this information or distort it in some way, they're going to get a bigger piece of the pie," he said. Emotional impediments can vary widely—fear, anger, depression—so it's important for lawyer negotiators to identify which one is causing the blockage and "address it through communication skills so that it will lighten up the negotiation."

Negotiation Tactics

Prior to becoming a mediator, Krivis was a trial lawyer for 10 years. "I was average," he said. "I didn't really have a special spark." But in 1989, one of his biggest clients brought in a mediator from Texas to work on the matter and Krivis was immediately hooked. During his years as a mediator, Krivis has seen ample evidence that lawyers don't take negotiations seriously enough. "What I've found with a lot of lawyers is that they're not prepared for negotiation," he said. "They jump in as though it's just another step in the process of going to court—but it's probably the most important step in the process because we know that 99 percent of cases get negotiated. "And when I say they don't prepare, I'm not saying that lightly. I'm very serious about that." Part of that preparation is to

Number of Lawyers Per Portion of the Population in Various Countries	
Country	**Number of Lawyers Per 100,000 People**
Austria	42
Belgium	112
Ecuador	93
Finland	24
Germany	92
Japan	30
Lithuania	16
Netherlands	68
Poland	63
Singapore	80
Slovakia	26
Spain	42
United Kingdom	138
United States	233
Compiled by editor.	

"put yourself in the other guy's shoes." For instance, if a lawyer is representing a plaintiff in an insurance dispute, Krivis said he should give a signal about the range in which his client intends to negotiate as a means of initiating a talk that could provide information about the opponent's position. "You need to find out what they're thinking, what they're anticipating, where they think they're headed," he said. "You need to anticipate what the other side is doing and where your client might be at the end of the negotiation so you have the ability to come in for a safe landing." He likens the art of negotiation to that of jazz musicianship. "You have to know the basic chords and elements of jazz, but you also have to be able to improvise. You have to kind of bob and weave and think on your feet with the idea of creating some kind of movement toward closure."

"A substantial number of mediations fail because of hostile and incompatible attorneys."

Conflict Resolution Does Not Always Avoid Lawsuits

Stephen R. Marsh

Stephen R. Marsh in the following viewpoint details the problems with conflict resolution, or mediation. Marsh acknowledges that alternative dispute resolution (ADR) can be effective under some circumstances, but he also highlights the main reasons why alternatives to lawsuits often fail. For instance, often the parties involved are not serious about mediation and only see it as a delaying tactic and in many instances, lawyers are not prepared for ADR. Stephen R. Marsh is a lawyer who writes about legal issues for a variety of sources.

As you read, consider the following questions:

1. According to the viewpoint, how often does mediation fail because of a lack of preparation?
2. How important is the concept of "good faith" in mediation, according to Marsh?

Stephen R. Marsh, "Mediation Pitfalls and Obstacles," *Alternative Dispute Resolution Resources*, 2003.

3. Which does Marsh contend is typically a faster process, arbitration or a legal trial?

There are times when mediation does not work. Many times, such cases are suitable for referral to arbitration. Other times it is just a matter of picking the right time to implement the process and the failure to work is a matter of timing or preparation rather than a matter of mediation being inappropriate. Finally, there are times when mediation will not work. This [viewpoint] . . . was written to identify the areas where (ADR) [alternative dispute resolution] in a matter will be frustrating and to help appreciate the areas in which ADR can still work as expected.

Procedural Problems

There are three extremely common procedural reasons reported by attorneys as reasons that mediations deadlocked.

- 24% of the failed mediations result from a lack of settlement authority. In a survey involving over 150 mediators and a substantial number of sessions, almost one quarter of the failures were the result of a necessary party not attending. Those with authority must attend in order for the process to work.

- 21% of the failed mediations result from a lack of preparation. Often referred to as an "inadequate discovery," the problems quite commonly reflect a party or an attorney who does not know enough about their own case to be able to settle the case.

- A substantial number of mediations fail because of hostile and incompatible attorneys. A mediation session is not the place for an aggressive, hostile and emotional attack on the other party or their attorney. Such attacks cause a substantial number of failed mediations.

Where one side is engaged in litigation with the primary intention of bleeding the other side with litigation expenses mediation is not fruitful. In this situation, a mediation session will generally be seen as one more opportunity to impose costs on the opposing party rather than a chance to cut costs and find a better resolution.

It is a primary tenant of mediation that the parties enter it in good faith. Malicious, bad faith litigation is a good example of the kind of bad faith that poisons the chances for success of mediation. Intellectual property conflicts are the same as any other in this regards, except that "bleeding" suits are more common.

Where an uninsured defendant faces catastrophic liquidity problems mediation will often be fruitless. [For instance] the defendant has $50,000,000 per year in sales of which $15,000,000.00 are from the sale of unlicensed properties. Assume that $5,000,000.00 per year would be the amount of royalties/etc. due (and not paid). Now assume the company has only $10,000,000.00 total in assets. (This is a situation that comes up commonly in print and art sales where a substantial portion of "public domain" prints in a catalog turn out to have current copyrights. Similar to this situation would be an uninsured motorist being sued . . . after a serious accident.)

A mediation session after three years of infringement (and $15,000,000.00, plus interest, in past due royalties) is unlikely to cause the defendant to bite the bullet. When the result of mediation requires the dissolution, reorganization or bankruptcy of a party, mediation usually does not generate the imminent pressure necessary to resolve the problem.

Note that in the same situation, mediation brought before a catastrophic loss looms can sometimes resolve some problems as will mediation brought after a judgment is entered in the case. In both cases, mediation serves as a supervised negotiation session where both parties can benefit. Mediation does not fail in such a situation, however it must be timed properly.

Most frustrating, is the situation where one side is mentally unable to appreciate the legitimacy or the limits of property rights. Thieves will rarely change their stripes and become trustworthy or legitimate just because they have entered a mediation session.

Individuals will differ, but a substantial portion of all intellectual property law litigation is against persons whose infringement is knowing and willful and who refuse to acknowledge property rights. Mediation with many of them is as fruitful as mediating with a burglar on the issue of his or her profession. However, there are successful mediation programs dealing with sentencing in criminal cases just as there is often successful mediation after judgment in intellectual property cases.

Arbitration

Arbitration often is faster than trial. However, arbitrators in many areas are rumored to be prone to "split the baby." If a party is entitled to harsh legal remedies and is willing to wait (and take some risk) in order to obtain them, then arbitration [is] thought to probably be dissatisfying. Many intellectual property law plaintiffs have basically written arbitration off because of the natural level of compromise that is perceived as to accompanying it. Note that this is an issue of perception.

Statistical studies do not bear this belief out—arbitrators are not likely to "split the baby." However, in seeking redress the choice of the arbitrator(s) is crucial, as is a review of the arbitrator(s)'s record and prior decisions.

Situations where one side is completely in the wrong, but is pushing arbitration or trial to obtain the benefit of natural compromise often do not result in fruitful mediation. If one side is unwilling to give an inch, and has no legal reason to

Public Perceptions of Lawyers and Mediation

There is considerable popular support for two propositions: too few disputes settle, and too many that do settle drag on for too long. There is likewise a widespread tendency to hold lawyers largely, if not exclusively, responsible for both problems. The popular belief—reflected in the [1994] Republican Contract With America, and the remarks of then Vice-President [Dan] Quayle to the American Bar Association—is that lawyers foment controversy and prolong litigation because they make money by doing so. The logic is simple and, for many politicians and voters, it is compelling.

Samuel Issacharoff, Charles Silver, and Kent D. Syverud,
"Bargaining Impediments and Settlement Behavior,"
Dispute Resolution: Bridging the Settlement Gap,
ed. D.A. Anderson. Greenwich, CT: JAI, 1996.
www.utexas.edu/law/faculty/csilver/class/DisputeResolution.htm.

compromise, non-binding arbitration or mediation have only about a break-even chance of persuading the other side to throw in the towel purely to save legal costs.

Mediation Can Work

There are times where mediation will work. After all, an 85% overall success rate reflects that there are many, many times that mediation will and does work.

In specific situations, the success rate is even higher than 85%.

Often, mediation also provides "one last chance" before major expenses are incurred. The general rule is that if negotiation can work, then mediation can make the negotiating process work better. If you are in a situation where negotiation won't work, mediation sometimes provides more of the "won't work" situation. However, mediation often finds creative alternatives that resolve the problems where negotiations have failed.

Even if you are unprepared, lack authority or are unreasonable in the extreme, mediation may help. However, it is best to increase your chances of success by not entering into mediation sessions with these problems.

ADR is an alternative. It remains an alternative because while it works most of the time, it cannot work all of the time.

However, unless your case fits into one of the special areas detailed above, negotiation, mediation and ADR ought to work for your conflicts just as well as they work for conflicts in every other realm of the law. ADR may be an alternative, but it is a generally good alternative.

Even in areas where most parties would not expect mediation to help, with proper evaluation (which mediation helps to create and improve), mediation often educates the parties and helps them to move forward. Thus mediation has been surprisingly successful in federal criminal prosecution and defense, in resolving federal business [temporary restraining order] requests (92% of the time), and has created a specialty in family law matters.

Being aware of the pitfalls and the opportunities, counsel can prepare to use this procedure, like any other tool available to counsel, to build a better case and to find a better resolution.

> "The mediation process is completely flexible and can be designed in a manner that meets the needs of the parties."

Conflict Resolution Strategies Are Reshaping the Legal System in a Positive Way

Karen L. Douglas

In the following viewpoint, Karen L. Douglas examines the alternative dispute resolution (ADR) policy that was adopted by the U.S. Air Force in 1999. The new policy was dubbed ADR First and was designed to limit the number of lawsuits brought against the Air Force by contractors and civilian employees. ADR First employs a range of options, from mediation to arbitration. The viewpoint explains the benefits of using alternatives to legal action for all parties involved in disputes. Karen L. Douglas is a lawyer and major in the U.S. Air Force who specializes in nontraditional conflict resolution.

As you read, consider the following questions:

1. As defined in the viewpoint, what is "facilitative mediation"?

Karen L. Douglas, "ADR for Air Force Contracts" *Contract Management*, vol. 45, December 2005, pp. 40–46. Copyright © 2005 National Contract Management Association. Reproduced by permission.

2. How do mini-trials operate under the air force's ADR First policy, according to the author?

3. According to Douglas, in the ADR First policy, who sets the outlines of the negotiations?

With the advent of the "ADR First" policy in 1999, U.S. Air Force contract dispute strategy evolved into a creative quest for mutually agreeable solutions without litigation. This strategic revolution was intended to foster better business relationships with contractors, increase remedy options beyond those available at trial, and substantially reduce the time necessary to resolve disputes.

Six years later, the Air Force's "ADR First" policy has achieved all of those goals and more, making ADR [alternative dispute resolution] the smart choice for contractors who are unhappy with a contracting officer's final decision. Never before have contractors enjoyed such an abundant variety of contract dispute resolution options that are geared toward achieving fair, expeditious, and inexpensive business solutions. . . .

The ADR modes that the Air Force employs include assisted negotiations at mediation and mini-trials, outcome prediction by early neutral evaluation and dispute review boards, non-binding arbitration, or binding arbitration by summary trial. The Armed Services Board of Contract Appeals [ASBCA] offers settlement judges for mini-trials, summary trials with binding decisions, and other structured ADR modes agreed upon by the board and parties.

Mediation

An assisted negotiation by mediation is an ADR forum aided by a neutral third party who has no stake in the result. This type of ADR is effective when the parties have "room to settle" but have been unsuccessful with traditional negotiations. The neutral third party is called a mediator; this mediator is not authorized to impose a settlement upon the parties but rather assists the parties in fashioning a mutually satisfactory solution to the controversy.

"Facilitative mediation" is the ADR technique in which the mediator simply facilitates discussions between or among the parties, without providing any form of evaluation of the merits of their respective positions. "Outcome prediction" and "evaluative mediation" are ADR modes in which the mediator (1) provides the parties with his/her views about the strengths and weaknesses of their respective positions, (2) opines as to potential outcome if the case were litigated, and (3) endeavors to help the parties fashion a mutually acceptable resolution to the controversy.

The Popularity of Mediation

Mediation is one of the most widely used ADR techniques in the private sector, as its flexibility and informality are useful for a wide variety of matters. In addition, mediation parties never surrender control of the ultimate resolution of their conflict. Contractors who are reluctant to lose control over the outcome of the disputed matter should be especially attracted to this form of ADR.

The mediation process is completely flexible and can be designed in a manner that meets the needs of the parties. Typically, it begins with an all-party joint meeting to share respective interests and positions. The process often includes a private session between the mediator and each party to allow further discussion of the case. At times, particularly when emotions run high, the mediator may choose to keep the parties separated and conduct "shuttle diplomacy." The mediator will work with the parties to identify common interests and to narrow the gap between the parties' respective positions.

The mediator serves to structure negotiations, acts as a catalyst between the parties, focuses the discussions, facilitates exchange between the parties, and assesses the positions taken by the parties during the course of the negotiations. In some cases, he/she may propose specific suggestions for settlement. In other cases, the mediator may guide the parties to generate more creative settlement proposals among themselves. During this time, the parties retain the power to resolve the issues through an informal, voluntary process. If a mutually agreeable settlement is possible, the mediator's role is to bring the parties to closure.

Early Neutral Evaluation

Early neutral evaluation (also referred to as "outcome prediction" or the "settlement judge" approach) has many of the same features as mediation. But, outcome prediction adds the neutral's review of the parties' positions and the information they provide. Furthermore, the neutral discloses his/her evaluation of the relative strengths and weaknesses of each party's position. These evaluations can be given to the parties individually or jointly. The early neutral evaluation/outcome prediction mode of ADR is a non-binding process. The parties generally select a neutral with subject-matter expertise whose opinion they respect—they frequently turn to the ASBCA judges to perform this function.

Mini-Trial

Despite the name, a mini-trial is not a small trial but rather a more structured process that includes the use of each of the party's senior principals. Mini-trials permit the parties to present their case (or an agreed-upon portion of the case) to their principals, who have authority to settle the issue in controversy. Often, these presentations are made with the assistance of a third-party neutral advisor, who might meet with the principals after the mini-trial to attempt to mediate a settlement. The neutral may also issue a formal written non-binding advisory opinion. The parties' ADR agreement can also provide for the limits of discovery for the proceeding.

Advantages of ADR

- ADR can be speedier [than a lawsuit]. A dispute can often be resolved in a matter of months, even weeks, through ADR, while a lawsuit can take years.

- ADR can save money. Court costs, attorney fees, and expert witness fees can be saved.

- ADR can permit more participation. With ADR, the parties may have more chances to tell their side of the story than in court and many have more control over the outcome.

- ADR can be flexible. The parties can choose the ADR process that's best for them.

- ADR can be cooperative. In mediation, for example, the parties having a dispute may work together with the neutral to resolve the dispute and agree to a remedy that makes sense to them, rather than work against each other.

Indiana Supreme Court,
"Alternative Dispute Resolution/Mediation,"
Self-Service Local Center.
www.in.gov/judiciary/selfservice/mediators.html.

The mini-trial presentation itself may be a summary or abbreviated hearing with or without verbal testimony. After the presentation, the principals often begin negotiations with the aid of the neutral as mediator or facilitator. The neutral's role is predefined by the written ADR agreement. The neutral generally presides at the presentation of the case, sets the ground rules, and as in other ADR actions, sees that the proceeding is conducted according to the ADR agreement. The neutral often has expertise in the federal rules of evidence and substantive law and may be called upon for advisory rulings on questions that are likely to arise if the matter proceeds to litigation. If the neutral has subject-matter expertise, then the agreement may also permit him or her to question presenters and witnesses. The neutral's learned questions can frequently focus the parties' attention on critical issues.

Because of the neutral's evidentiary rule and substantive law expertise, the mini-trial ADR mechanism is excellent for resolving factual issues or mixed questions of law and fact. Furthermore, this ADR technique highlights the strengths and weaknesses of the case. Settlement authority for mini-trials is the same as for negotiated settlements. At the conclusion of the mini-trial presentation, the decision-making principals usually adjourn to negotiate the matter. The neutral may be called upon to act as advisor, mediator, or fact-finder in this subsequent session, depending upon the terms of the ADR agreement and what the parties want.

Arbitration

Arbitration is an issue resolution process, whereby a neutral third party is empowered by agreement of the parties to issue a decision on the controversy. In this process, the neutral is called an arbitrator. Arbitration is commonly used in the private sector, and the decision can be either binding or nonbinding, according to the ADR agreement. A binding ADR would be one in which the proceeding results in a decision that is final and conclusive—it may not be appealed or set aside, absent a showing of fraud.

There are significant legal restrictions on binding ADR within the DOD [Department of Defense]. The only binding ADR method available to the air force is summary trial before an ASBCA judge. The DOD is not authorized to use binding ADR proceedings unless the arbitrator is an ASBCA judge.

Summary Trial with Binding Decision

A summary trial with a binding decision permits the parties to expedite the appeal schedule and to try their appeal informally before an administrative judge or panel of judges. The greatest distinguishing feature between an ASBCA trial and an ADR summary trial before the ASBCA is that, in a summary trial, the parties design the trial process (format, timing, rules, etc.) with the assistance of a judge who is often selected by the parties. Generally, the parties elect to have one judge decide the case, submit pre-hearing position papers (instead of post-hearing briefs), and opt for more streamlined evidentiary presentations. The judge(s) will issue a verbal "bench" decision shortly after conclusion of the proceeding, followed later by a summary written decision.

Under most circumstances, the nearly immediate decision upon conclusion of the trial is one of the greatest advantages of the ADR summary trial process. By comparison, a traditional ASBCA trial judgment is rendered only after the parties submit post-trial and reply briefs, the two other judges review the trial record and briefs, and the three judges then agree on a written decision. It is difficult to determine how long this process will take, but it customarily exceeds a year. Furthermore, under traditional ASBCA trials, the trial decision can still be appealed, thus delaying certainty on the matter for years. The decision by an ASBCA judge in a binding summary trial is rendered almost immediately upon the trial's conclusion and cannot be appealed, thus providing expeditious finality to the controversy.

Parties Make the Rules

One of the great benefits of selecting ADR is the parties' ability to set the parameters of the proceedings to suit their goals. The ADR agreement can encompass a great variety of issues and results in a tailor-made resolution plan. At the parties' agreement, ADR ranges from utterly informal meetings to formal procedures modeled on actual trial. Discovery rules are drafted by the parties and set within their comfort levels. The location of the ADR proceeding, opportunity for *ex-parte* communications, and use of evidence is up to the decision of the parties. ADR results are not binding precedent, and if the parties wish, there are no written transcripts of the proceedings to influence future dealings among the parties. Because ADR is so flexible, these proceedings lend themselves to a wide variety of presentation technology, including teleconferencing and virtual courtroom videoconferencing.

The distribution of ADR costs is negotiable in an ADR agreement, as well as Equal Access to Justice Act lawyers' fees for those qualifying contractors whose ADR results in an order of settlement. Issue resolution by ADR isn't an all-or-nothing proposition. The parties may decide to resolve only a portion of a claim by ADR and litigate the other issues, or may decide to resolve multiple claims all in one ADR. And, perhaps best of all, ADR almost always resolves both entitlement and quantum awards [damages] at the same time.

If ADR Fails, the Contractor Is Still No Worse Off

A contractor's right to appeal a decision to the ASBCA is not compromised by attempting ADR, unless, of course, the parties agree to this as a term of the ADR agreement. If an appeal is pending before the ASBCA and the parties elect to try conflict resolution by ADR, then the ASBCA grants a suspension of the proceedings for ADR resolution. If a non-binding ADR proceeding fails to resolve the dispute, then the ASBCA simply restores the appeal to the active docket, and there are no strategic reasons for a party to avoid ADR in order to protect its case. The ASBCA's rules are promulgated to promote candid participation by the parties, since neutral advisors and settlement judges who participated in an ADR that failed to settle are ordinarily recused from participation in a trial on that same matter, unless the parties specifically request otherwise and the ASBCA chair approves the request. Likewise, the AS-BCA neutral may not discuss the ADR case with any other board personnel.

Furthermore, most ADR agreements include a confidentiality clause which prevents any matters submitted at an ADR from coming back to haunt the parties at subsequent trial. Under such confidentiality clauses and applicable law, any written material prepared specifically for ADR, any verbal presentations made at an ADR proceeding, and any discussions between the parties during ADR are inadmissible in any future board proceeding. Conversely, the parties aren't faced with the dilemma of "if-you-use-it-then-you-lose-it," since evidence otherwise admissible at trial is not rendered inadmissible because of its use at an ADR proceeding.

> *"Can a justice system dedicated to con-*
> *ciliation rather than adjudication of*
> *facts and law maintain its status as a*
> *third branch of government?"*

Conflict Resolution Strategies Are Reshaping the Legal System in a Negative Way

Deborah Hensler

In the viewpoint that follows, Deborah Hensler criticizes alterna-
tive dispute resolution (ADR) policies and techniques for the ef-
fect they have on the American legal system. The author asserts
that increased use of ADR will likely lead to higher legal costs, as
well as a less efficient system for mediating disagreements. In ad-
dition, Hensler contends that ADR is increasingly undermining
the constitutional role of courts in the American political system.
Deborah Hensler is a noted legal scholar and the John W. Ford
Professor of Dispute Resolution at Stanford Law School in Cali-
fornia.

Deborah Hensler, "Our Courts, Ourselves: How the Alternative Dispute Resolution Movement Is Reshaping Our Legal System," *Penn State Law Review*, vol. 108, 2003, pp. 165–97. Copyright © 2003 by The Penn State Dickinson School of Law. Reproduced by permission of the author.

As you read, consider the following questions:

1. How can alternative dispute resolution raise the public costs of litigation, according to the viewpoint?

2. As stated in the viewpoint, have courts and legislatures embraced or rejected ADR?

3. Why does the author argue that the "public spectacle of civil litigation" is important to see?

There is little evidence that jurists who have embraced . . . [the] new visions of the courts have carefully considered their institutional implications. Should generalist judges lead courts dedicated to social harmony, problem solving and self-understanding? Or would such courts be better led by communication experts, risk management specialists, and counseling psychologists? What role should the public play in selecting the experts who will shape the new dispute resolution process? Can a justice system dedicated to conciliation [agreement] rather than adjudication [judgment] of facts and law maintain its status as a third branch of government, equal to the legislature and executive? Whatever their failures in achieving efficient and fair justice for citizens, the core competence of today's courts is adjudication. Re-imagining the purpose of courts requires re-thinking their institutional structure as well.

The Courts and Conflict Resolution

Just where we are in the story of the alternative dispute resolution [ADR] movement—whether we are nearing the concluding chapter or still in mid-narrative, with many turns in the plot line still to come—is not clear. But some parts of the story seem clear. There is little evidence that neighborhood justice centers have substantially reduced urban social conflict or contributed to a significant redistribution of power within communities, although they may well be helping neighbors work out minor disputes. There is little evidence that alternative dispute resolution procedures within courts have reduced

© 2002 Larry Wright, The Detroit News, and PoliticalCartoons.com

the average time to dispose of civil lawsuits, or the average public or private expense to litigate cases in a system that has long relied on settlement rather than adjudication to resolve most cases. There is also little evidence that alternative dispute resolution procedures outside of courts have reduced the transaction costs of resolving conflicts that would never have gone to trial anyway, although they may be contributing to a drop in civil case filings. By precluding jury trial, private binding arbitration may well have decreased the expected value of a dispute outcome, but any savings accruing from this may be outweighed by an increase in claiming, if arbitration simplifies the dispute process for ordinary consumers or employees. Whether alternative dispute resolution processes outside or within courts have significantly increased the preexisting imbalance of power between the "haves" and "have nots" is unclear. While there are reasons to believe that ADR sometimes disadvantages the less powerful, the traditional litigation process may not do much better in creating a level playing field.

If lawyers succeed in shaping alternative dispute resolution procedures to comport with traditional notions of settlement, the immediate outcomes of the dispute resolution movement may simply be to increase the costs of litigation by substituting paid lawyer-settlers for publicly subsidized judge-settlers. The story of the alternative dispute resolution movement might then appear to be just a very old tale, retold.

But I find it hard to believe that the myriad new statutes and court rules promoting or mandating private dispute resolution, the thousands of mediator training sessions, promotional videotapes, and educational programs, and the public rhetoric that has accompanied all of these will have so little long-term consequence. To encourage people to consider alternatives to litigation, in federal and state courts nationwide, judges and mediators are telling claimants that legal norms are antithetical [in opposition] to their interests, that vindicating their legal rights is antithetical to social harmony, that juries are capricious [impulsive], that judges cannot be relied upon to apply the law properly, and that it is better to seek inner peace than social change. To drive these messages home, courts and legislatures mandate mediation, preclude dissemination of information about what transpires during mediation sessions, and—in the case of binding arbitration—sharply limit the ability of claimants to challenge the process or outcome. Moreover, both legislatures and courts display a breezy indifference to the qualifications of those who act as third-party neutrals and to the costs imposed on litigants by alternative dispute resolution mandates—all apparently based on the belief that any alternative to adversarial conflict must be beneficial.

ADR and Changes to Legal System

Looking backwards, we may well come to view the dispute resolution movement as contributing to—if not creating—a profound change in our view of the justice system. With increasing barriers to litigating, fewer citizens will find their own way into court (although they may be brought there to

answer criminal charges). Those who are not barred from using the courts by contractual agreement will increasingly find
themselves shepherded outside the courthouse to confidential
conferences presided over by private neutrals in private ven-
ues. With little experience of public adjudication and little information available about the process or outcomes of dispute
resolution, citizens' abilities to use the justice system effectively to achieve social change will diminish markedly. Sur-
rounded by a culture that celebrates social harmony and self-
realization and disparages social conflict—whatever its causes
or aims—citizens' tendencies to turn to the court as a vehicle
for social transformation will diminish as well. Over the long
run, all of the doors of the multi-door courthouse may swing
outward.

The Impact of ADR

Why should we care? If disputes are resolved efficiently in private, by private individuals and organizations, if conflict is
avoided and citizens learn to seek compromise when disputes
do arise, won't society be better off? Leaving aside the still un-
answered question about whether private dispute resolution
is, in fact, more efficient than public dispute resolution, and
the considerable evidence that in most circumstances people
already avoid conflict by compromising or "learning to live
with" life's misfortunes and unfairness, I think the answer is
"no." . . .

The public spectacle of civil litigation gives life to the "rule
of law." To demonstrate that the law's authority can be mobi-
lized by the least powerful as well as the most powerful in society, we need to observe employees and consumers successfully suing large corporations and government agencies,
minority group members successfully suing majority group
members, and persons engaged in unpopular activities establishing their legal rights to continue those activities.

Dispute resolution behind closed doors precludes such observation. In a democracy where many people are shut out of legislative power either because they are too few in number, or too dispersed to elect representatives, or because they do not have the financial resources to influence legislators, collective litigation in class or other mass form provides an alternative strategy for group action. Private individualized dispute resolution extinguishes the possibility of such collective litigation. Conciliation has much to recommend it. But the visible presence of institutionalized and legitimized conflict, channeled productively, teaches citizens that it is not always better to compromise and accept the status quo because, sometimes, great gains are to be had by peaceful contest.

"High-profile, wealthy clients such as ... celebrities Brad Pitt and Jennifer Aniston have turned to private judges for their divorce settlements."

Private Conflict Resolution Can Be More Effective than the Public Court System

Sheila Nagaraj

In the following viewpoint, Sheila Nagaraj explores the growing trend of private judges in states such as California. Private judges are often able to handle cases much more quickly than the public court system and this leads to lower legal costs for people involved in litigation, she says. In addition, private judges allow people a much higher degree of privacy than the traditional legal system, a factor that has made them very attractive to celebrities. Sheila Nagaraj is a lawyer and law clerk in the United States District Court in the Southern District of New York.

As you read, consider the following questions:

1. What is private judging, according to the viewpoint?

Sheila Nagaraj, "The Marriage of Family Law and Private Judging in California," *Yale Law Journal*, vol. 116, May 2007, pp. 1615–1623.

2. What are the main differences between a private judge and an arbitrator, as stated in the viewpoint?

3. What does Nagaraj claim is the most controversial aspect of private judging?

As court officials, legal assistance professionals, and policy-makers work to ensure open access to an overwhelmed public judicial system, a new—and some say dangerous—brand of justice has quietly emerged in the United States. Private judging is a hybrid of traditional litigation and alternative dispute resolution. After consent by all parties and an order from the presiding judge of a public court, the parties may appoint a private decision-maker, usually a retired judge, who hears the parties' arguments and then issues a binding opinion. In some jurisdictions—including California, where private judging was born and has principally developed—these private judges are vested with the authority of public judges, are subject to most of the same legal constraints, and issue judgments that are directly appealable. But like arbitrators, private judges promise speedy, confidential decision-making.

Private judging fills a particularly worrisome gap between public adjudication and arbitration in the family law context. Though such cases often demand the privacy and convenience of arbitration, major issues of family law, including divorce and custody disputes, are off-limits to arbitrators. Thus far, only divorces have been sent to private judges in California. As one author has noted, however, other family disputes are similarly well suited to private judging because few parties are involved and the issues are rarely of public significance.

Instead of being viewed as a "best of both worlds" approach, however, private judging has suffered sharp criticism as it has grown in popularity. Its greatest draw—the confidentiality it offers the parties—is also its most fervently disputed characteristic. Private trials inherently afford litigants a greater degree of privacy because of their limited accessibility to the public and the media. Allegations that some private judges abuse the system and shield information that should be made public have made such enhanced privacy all the more contentious.

Despite the controversy surrounding private judges, S.B. 1015, a [Senate] bill introduced in the California state legislature, would increase the authority of all judges—including private judges—to further conceal the mechanics of legal proceedings that should be publicly accessible. In light of this legislation and the concerns it raises, I propose a unique solution for private judging that harnesses its privacy and efficiency benefits and simultaneously works toward eliminating its ethical difficulties. I call for the regulation and limited expansion of private judging in the family law context, so as to benefit those who can afford private judges and to help alleviate the burden on public judicial resources. . . .

Private Judges and Family Law

Thirty years after the inception of private adjudication in California, private judges hear cases on a variety of issues, but more than half of the cases involve family disputes. Private judges are seen to be useful in family law cases that require the knowledge, expertise, and power of a traditional judge, but in which the parties seek the efficiency and immediacy of an arbitrator. High-profile, wealthy clients such as billionaire Ronald Burkle and celebrities Brad Pitt and Jennifer Aniston have turned to private judges for their divorce settlements.

While many authors use "arbitrator" and "private judge" interchangeably, I draw on the important distinctions between the two under California law. First, private judges must be members of the state bar, while there are no restrictions on who may serve as an arbitrator. Second, whereas parties may submit their dispute to an arbitrator without any approval from the court, a private judge may be appointed only after the case has been filed in court and the presiding judge has agreed to send the case to a private judge. Third, the merits of an arbitrator's award (on questions of both law and fact) are unreviewable by a court except in narrow cases as provided by statute. By contrast, the decisions of private judges are directly appealable.

Perhaps the most crucial difference is that in California, as well as in several other states, arbitrators have been barred from adjudicating most family disputes. Case law suggests that arbitrators are excluded from this area because they are not bound by legal precedent and because their decisions are unreviewable, in the New York case of *Glauber v. Glauber* [1993], for instance, the court held that child custody disputes are unsuitable for arbitration due to public policy concerns. Private judging, however, does not raise such concerns. Its hybrid nature bridges the gap between public adjudication and arbitration, offering a better forum for resolving family law disputes.

Private Judges Versus Arbitrators

Unlike arbitrators, private judges bring the accountability and experience of public judging to family law cases. Because private judges are held to the same expectations as public judges, they may be ordered to consider such legal standards as the "best interests of the child," and their decisions may be reviewed if they fail to do so. In addition, private judges will likely have had years of experience as public judges adjudicating family disputes. Parties can select a mutually agreeable private judge who has specialized knowledge of the relevant area of family law, such as custody, property division, or alimony. This may lead to greater confidence that the end result will be fair to all interested parties and may therefore reduce the likelihood of appeals that could further clog up the public judiciary.

Moreover, unlike public judges, private judges bring the convenience, efficiency, and confidentiality of arbitration to family law disputes. Private judging offers litigants a remarkable degree of flexibility: because they need not rely on the availability of public judges and courtrooms, the parties can tailor the proceedings to their own schedules. Private adjudication also promises prompt resolution of disputes, as private judges have lighter caseloads and can devote more time to individual cases. Given that divorce and custody battles can drag on for months to the detriment of all the relationships involved, speed and efficiency are invaluable. In fact, despite the outrageously high fees that some private judges command, private adjudication may result in lower costs to the parties because quick resolution substantially reduces attorneys' fees.

Most importantly, private judging affords family law litigants the confidentiality and privacy that the public court system cannot provide. Observers of the process agree that, together with efficiency, privacy is the most highly valued aspect of private judging because it shields parties' sensitive information, such as financial records and custody arrangements. Private hearings may also be more conducive to reaching satisfactory settlements because they lack the adversarial nature of public trials. This is of particular importance in family law disputes, as a less adversarial environment can foster more constructive family relationships once a case has been decided.

Notably, private judging does not only benefit litigants who are wealthy enough to afford it. As public court administrators and officials struggle to cope with budget cuts, longer trials, and a shortage of well-trained staff, an ever-growing number of litigants are forced to choose between settling a case and waiting perhaps years for their day in court. Private judging helps these less affluent litigants gain access to the courts. In California, for instance, though family cases represented only 7.5% of total filings in 2004–2005, they accounted for nearly a third of the trial courts' workload in terms of time. Shifting some of these cases to private judges would benefit individuals of all economic classes by alleviating the burden on the publicly financed judiciary and allowing greater access to the public legal system.

The Drawbacks of Private Judging

Confidentiality is not only private judging's greatest benefit, but also its most controversial feature. Although California law requires that the public be allowed to attend all civil proceedings, hearings in front of a private judge are typically more private than traditional court proceedings. The fact that these cases are heard outside of a courtroom and often on private property renders them far less accessible to the public. There also is no statutory requirement that a court reporter transcribe the proceedings. While private adjudication therefore offers a privacy-protective option for family disputes—which can only approximate the confidentiality offered by arbitrators' sealing of records—critics charge that such privacy is in fact excessive and dangerous secrecy.

The introduction of S.B. 1015 has only reignited controversy, as it would allow all judges greater latitude in sealing or redacting portions of court records. The bill has also brought greater media attention to alleged abuses by private judges. Newspaper articles have reported that some documents are never placed in the appropriate court files and that proceedings, held in offices or even in hotel rooms, are hidden from interested observers. As increasing numbers of celebrities seek out private judges precisely because of the secrecy they offer, critics have raised constitutional concerns about expanding private judging.

The secrecy that private adjudication provides is all the more troubling to critics because, as the presiding judge of the Los Angeles Superior Court has noted, it can be difficult to prod private judges into following the rules. For example, private judge Stephen Lachs, who presided over Michael Jackson's divorce, had his decision overturned after he barred a reporter from a hearing and his case files were found to be incomplete.

Retired judges cannot be disciplined by California's Commission on Judicial Performance, and private judges therefore operate without public supervision and safeguards.

A final concern is that private adjudication will create a two-tiered system of justice that benefits the wealthy at the expense of others. California Chief Justice Ronald M. George has analogized the potential divide between public and private judging to that between public and private schools, and he has suggested that the large-scale expansion of private judging might lead to the perception of a stratified legal system. Only the poor and the middle class would have a stake in the public courts, while the wealthy would enjoy their own brand of justice.

A New Model for Private Judging

Despite abundant criticism, private judging is only growing in popularity. Rather than reject this institution wholesale, I propose a unique solution for the family law context that harnesses private judging's privacy and efficiency benefits while limiting its drawbacks. My proposal would be enacted in the form of a statutory provision, which would include the following central elements.

First, the statute would, at least initially, limit the scope of private judging to family law issues. Restricting the pool of cases that private judges may adjudicate would make it easier to regulate their conduct as well as to prevent potential abuses of the system. Moreover, while much of the debate over private judging has focused on confidentiality, such controversy is diminished in the family law context. The public has less need to know about the intimate details of a couple's divorce proceeding than about other civil matters, and, because children are often involved in family law proceedings, a primary goal of such proceedings must be to safeguard their interests and privacy. The coupling of the sensitive nature of family law cases and the fact that many of these cases do not raise issues of public concern makes family law the perfect "test tube" environment for private judging.

Of course, private judges should not be able to abuse their powers in the name of protecting privacy. Therefore, a second prong of the statute would implement a canon of ethics designed to limit privacy to an appropriate level and to hold judges accountable for their decisions. It would ensure that licensed private judges would, among other things: agree to uphold and apply all relevant legal standards when deciding cases; provide a written judicial opinion for a decision at any party's request; and arrange for a reporter to transcribe the entirety of the proceedings in certain cases, such as those involving custody disputes. To protect the parties' privacy (to a limited degree), the record would omit the names and identifying information of children, as well as confidential financial information.

Third, private judges would hear cases that were time-consuming only because of procedural complications. Public judges would still adjudicate any case that presented novel substantive legal questions. Moreover, it would be within the public judge's discretion to determine whether a particular family law case that presented no novel issues of law but contained complicated facts should be handled by a public or private judge.

A final prong of the state would address the fear that private judging might lead to a two-tiered justice system, by requiring each private judge to contribute a percentage of her fees to a government fund. These contributions would primarily cover the administrative costs of the private judging system (such as redacting confidential information from records), but a significant portion would be put back into the public court system to help implement desperately needed improvements. The special costs of private family law proceedings make them specially suited to such a fee structure. For instance, while an average divorce proceeding lasts about one

The Lure of Private Judging

In recent years, the demand for private judges has soared.

Today, the American Arbitration Association and several other arbitration providers compete to hire the biggest names on the bench.

Although arbitrators need not be judges, or even lawyers, most are. And former judges are preferred because "lawyers don't trust each other," says Lucie Barron, head of Action Dispute Resolution Services in Los Angeles.

The attractions for judges are obvious. A Superior Court judge earns $133,055 a year, while top arbitrators can make $10,000 or more a day, in addition to retirement pay.

Reynolds Holding,
"Judges' Action Cast Shadow on Integrity of Court,"
San Francisco Chronicle, *October 9, 2001.*

year, with an estimated cost of $15,000, Michael Jackson's divorce case lasted ten days, and the private judge earned $73,000. Funds collected from the private judging system could go a long way toward alleviating the state justice system's financial difficulties and increasing access and efficiency for individuals filing in the public courts.

The Future of Private Judging

The future of private adjudication in the United States is still taking shape. As the media spotlight shines more intensely on the rich and famous, wealthy clients will go to greater lengths to shield what they consider to be intimate details of their private lives. Meanwhile, the courts must continue to balance these privacy to interests with the right of public access to court proceedings. The reforms I propose may improve the state of private *and* public justice, while ensuring that the judicial system continues to comport with basic notions of fairness and equality.

> "Adjudication results in win-lose out-
> comes, leaving little chance the parties
> will develop a collaborative or integra-
> tive solution."

Private Conflict Resolution Is Not Necessarily More Effective than the Court System

Brad Spangler

In the following viewpoint, Brad Spangler compares the benefits of public alternative dispute resolution (ADR) to private conflict resolution, such as the fact that public ADR decisions can be appealed, unlike private settlements. In addition, judges in the court system are held to a set of publicly known qualifications, which is not always the case in private ADR efforts. The viewpoint also asserts that there is more consistency in public ADR than in the private sector. Brad Spangler studies public policy dispute resolution for the research institution Resolve in Washington, D.C.

As you read, consider the following questions:

1. Who does the author argue has control of the alternative dispute resolution (ADR), the clients or the lawyers?

Brad Spangler, "Adjudication," *Beyond Intractability*, eds. by Guy Burgess and Heidi Burgess. July 2003. www.beyondintractability.org/essay/adjudication.

2. According to the viewpoint, is ADR more or less expensive than traditional court cases?

3. Do traditional courts work for all conflicts or disputes, according to Spangler?

A djudication generally refers to processes of decision making that involve a neutral third party with the authority to determine a binding resolution through some form of judgment or award. Adjudication is carried out in various forms, but most commonly occurs in the court system. It can also take place outside the court system in the form of alternative dispute resolution [ADR] processes such as *arbitration*, private judging, and mini-trials. However, court-based adjudication is usually significantly more formal than arbitration and other ADR processes. The development of the field of alternative dispute resolution has led many people to use the term *adjudication* to refer specifically to litigation or conflicts addressed in court. Therefore, court-based adjudication will be the main focus of this essay.

Adjudication

Adjudication is an involuntary, adversarial process. This means arguments are presented to prove one side right and one side wrong, resulting in win-lose outcomes. In civil cases, one side/ person that believes he or she has been wronged (plaintiff) files legal charges against another (defendant). In other words, somebody sues someone they have a legal problem with. Once this occurs, both parties are obligated by law to participate in court-based proceedings. If the case goes to trial, each side then presents reasoned arguments and evidence to support their claims. Once that presentation of evidence and arguments is completed, a judge or jury then makes a decision. Appeals may be filed in an attempt to get a higher court to reverse the decision. If no appeal is filed, the decision is binding on both parties.

Arbitration and Secrecy

Arbitration is frequently conducted pursuant to confidentiality rules and agreements that can conceal the existence and substance of a dispute, the identities of the parties, and the resolution of the controversy. Mediation proceedings, frequently cloaked with an evidentiary privilege, are accorded even more privacy. Public policy strongly encourages alternative dispute resolution, and courts and legislatures unquestioningly assume that confidentiality is essential to its efficient and effective functioning. In contrast to litigation, then, ADR largely operates in an "environment of secrecy" whose "closed doors can mask a world of mischief."

Laurie Itratky Doré, "Public Courts Versus Private Justice: It's Time to Let Some Sun Shine in on Alternative Dispute Resolution," Chicago-Kent Law Review, vol. 81, September 2006. http://lawreview.kentlaw.edu/articles/81-2/dore.pdf.

Disadvantages of Court-Based Adjudication

The alternative dispute resolution movement of the 1970s and 1980s was based primarily on promoting alternatives to litigation and court-based resolution procedures. ADR advocates argued that alternative processes such as *mediation* and arbitration were more effective and constructive, among other reasons, than litigation. Though the debate over which form of justice is "better" is still ongoing, adjudication definitely does have some negative qualities or disadvantages. Some of the main criticisms of court-based adjudication include:

- Court-based adjudication is prohibitively expensive in terms of monetary cost, making it impossible for some parties to take their complaints to a court of law.

- Control of the process is removed from the client/ disputant and delegated to the lawyer and the court.

- The decision makers lack expertise in the area of the dispute. In most courts the judges are generalists and practically every jury is too.

- Court dockets are often overbooked, causing significant delays before a case is heard. In the meantime, the un- resolved issues can cause serious problems for the dis- putants.

- Litigation requires that people's problems be translated into legal issues, yet the court's decision about those issues does not always respond to the real nature of the underlying problem. For example, issues might be framed in terms of money, where the real issue is one of trust and respect . . . emotional issues not dealt with in an adversarial process.

- In addition, courts are constrained by the law as to what solutions they can offer. When the underlying issues are not addressed, the decision may produce a short-term settlement, but not a long-term resolution.

- Adjudication results in win-lose outcomes, leaving little chance the parties will develop a collaborative or inte- grative solution to the problem, unless the case is settled out of court before the trial.

- Litigation often drives parties apart because of its ad- versarial, positional nature, while effective resolution often requires that they come closer together. This po- larization of the disputants is also often accompanied by emotional distress.

- People enmeshed in litigation experience indirect costs beyond the legal fees. For example, disruption to the functioning of one's business or progression of one's career can be just as damaging.

Some conflicts cannot be resolved in court, because there is no court with clear jurisdiction that is accepted by all the parties involved. This happens most often in international conflicts when one or more parties refuses to honor the authority of any international court (such as the International Criminal Court or the International Court of Justice).

Advantages of Adjudication/Litigation

Though adjudication is an adversarial process, it can produce some clear benefits over other options for dispute resolution (i.e., ADR). Proponents of adjudication argue that the process produces more fair and consistent decisions than alternative dispute resolution processes. In fact, ADR has been criticized as providing "second-class justice." This allegation is based on the fact that processes like mediation have not been institutionalized and there are no set standards of practice or rules of law upon which they are based. On the other hand, adjudication or litigation is grounded in the public judicial system and has a vast array of rules and regulations. There are several advantages that adjudication advocates cite when promoting this dispute settlement process:

- Adjudication produces an imposed, final decision that the parties are obligated to respect. An alternative process, such as mediation, produces only voluntary agreements that can easily fail.

- The outcomes of litigation are, without exception, binding and enforceable. Although arbitration decisions can be binding and enforceable (with the backing of the judicial system) this only occurs when the participating parties agree to such parameters. A party who has not agreed to arbitrate cannot be forced to do so, or be bound by the outcome of arbitration between other parties. With court-based adjudication, however, participation is involuntary and all outcomes are binding and enforceable. This can be a true advantage in situations where there is a serious lack of trust and/or respect between the parties.

- The use of court-based adjudication or litigation allows for decisions to be appealed. The option to appeal confers multiple benefits. For example in monetary settlements, the winning party is often willing to renegotiate the settlement before it goes to appeal so as to avoid full reversal and retrial. Appeals also allow the reversal of incorrect decisions. Sometimes mistakes are made or evidence that was clearly prejudicial was allowed, thus tarnishing what otherwise may have been a just outcome.

- Public adjudication offers procedural safeguards that ensure parties due process under the law. Among such safeguards are cross-examination, limitations on hearsay and other rules of evidence, pre-hearing mandatory sharing of information between sides, and other statutory and constitutional protections that fall under the umbrella of due process. Procedural stipulations such as these help ensure that adjudicated outcomes will be fair.

- Litigated decisions are authoritative and based on precedent.

- Court-based decisions are, in theory, based on principles of the law (established norms) that have been previously validated. This makes for consistency in how similar cases are decided over time and better predictability regarding the range of possible outcomes.

- Court-based adjudication is institutionalized, meaning that a party with a complaint needs no one's permission to bring a lawsuit against another party. In addition, since the courts are funded by the government and do not rely on customer satisfaction (as do some ADR providers), they can issue decisions that may be disliked by the parties, without fear of reprisal in any form.

• Judges, the ultimate adjudicative decision makers, are chosen through a variety of publicly known procedures that ensure they are qualified for the job.

• In addition, there are cases where settlement of a short-term dispute is all that is needed or possible. (Here "settlement" is being compared to *resolution* which is deeper and more lasting.) If there is no need for or no possibility of a future relationship between the parties, a settlement of their dispute is adequate. If relationships are going to be a long-term issue, however, resolution is preferable, when possible. When not, dispute settlement may well be better than continued fighting, and arbitration is a way to obtain such settlement.

Periodical Bibliography

The following articles have been selected to supplement the diverse views presented in this chapter.

Pat Broderick
"Defusing Disputes: National Conflict Resolution Center Seeks Solutions to Variety of Problems and Issues," *San Diego Business Journal*, March 7, 2005.

Nan Waller Burnett and Sally K. Ortner
"The Holistic Practice of Conflict Resolution," *Colorado Lawyer*, December 2006.

Janice F. Caramanica
"Resolving Conflict: Alternative Dispute Resolution Helps Avoid Formal Complaints," *State Magazine*, January 2007.

Paul Davis
"Conflict Resolution: Six Secrets to Successfully Conquer Conflicts," *Contract Management*, September 2006.

Yuval Eylon and Alon Harel
"The Right to Judicial Review," *Virginia Law Review*, September 2006.

Gerald W. Ghikas
"Making Commercial Arbitration Work: Reaping the Benefits, Avoiding the Pitfalls," *Oil Week Magazine*, April 2006.

Ariel N. Lavinbuk
"The Outsourcing of American Law," *Slate*, August 15, 2006.

Edward Marshall
"Choose to Avoid or Escalate Conflict—or Opt for Resolution," *Triangle Business Journal*, October 28, 2005.

Michael Orey
"The Vanishing Trial," *Business Week*, April 30, 2007.

Pensions Management
"Trustee Conflicts-Conflict and Resolution," December 1, 2005.

CHAPTER 3

Is Conflict Resolution the Best Way to Solve Environmental Problems?

Chapter Preface

In the United States and around the world, people increasingly struggle over the control of natural resources. Water, arable land, and minerals have long been the source of competition, but strife has expanded as the world's population has grown and factors such as global warming and the loss of biodiversity have limited many natural resources. Politicians, scientists, and even celebrities have called for action to address these issues. For instance, Arizona senator and 2008 Republican presidential candidate John McCain declared that the United States "has both an obligation and self-interest in facing head-on the serious environmental, economic and national security threat posed by global warming."

Water is a resource that is often at the core of environmental disputes. Throughout the world, more than 470 billion gallons of water are drawn from the ground or lakes and rivers each day. That is more than 11 billion barrels or more than 165 times the number of barrels of oil pumped each day. Nonetheless, that amount is not enough to provide the world's population with sanitary water for drinking and other personal uses. Only about two-thirds of the world's population has adequate access to potable water. In 2006 alone, there were five worldwide conflicts over control of water that resulted in the loss of life, including fighting in Somalia over water in which more than 250 died in what became known as the "war of the wells."

Some argue that one means to prevent fighting and to better preserve resources is to share control of natural resources or at least allow governments and environmental organizations a higher degree of influence in managing the nation's environment. One possible way to reduce tensions over resources and better accomplish the goal of more equitable distribution is through alternative dispute resolution or conflict resolution.

Advocates of conflict resolution strategies argue that these techniques allow environmental disputes to be solved more quickly than traditional legal or political processes. Proponents also contend that alternative dispute resolution provides the optimum means by which competing interests can be reconciled. In other words, it is the best way to ensure that everyone's concerns and needs are taken into account when crafting a settlement over environmental issues.

The authors in the following viewpoints examine the role of conflict resolution strategies in environmental disputes. The essays by scholars, journalists, and writers examine whether or not alternative dispute resolution is an appropriate means to solve environmental conflicts and how the strategies should, or should not, be implemented.

"Dispute resolution cannot replace the political process, but it can supplement it."

Environmental Conflict Resolution Allows for a Balance of Competing Interests

Jeffrey P. Cohn

In the viewpoint that follows, author Jeffrey P. Cohn presents examples of environmental conflict resolution (ECR) while examining the positive and negative aspects of ECR and the history of alternative environmental dispute resolution. While ECR has been important in several settlements, states Cohn, federal agencies also have experienced problems with the approach, especially when groups attempt to gain political or legal advantages in their disputes. Jeffrey P. Cohn is a writer who specializes in science and environmental matters.

Jeffrey P. Cohn, "Environmental Conflict Resolution," *Bioscience*, vol. 52, May 2004, pp. 400–405. Copyright © 2004 Bioscience. Republished with permission of Bioscience, conveyed through Copyright Clearance Center, Inc.

As you read, consider the following questions:

1. According to the viewpoint, what federal action created a controversy in the Humboldt-Toiyabe National Forest in Nevada?

2. According to the author, what is one way in which individuals or groups abuse environmental conflict resolution?

3. Approximately how many cases does the viewpoint state the U.S. Institute for Environmental Conflict Resolution has managed since 1999?

A dispute over a storm-damaged road in the Humboldt-Toiyabe National Forest in northeastern Nevada had all the signs of becoming ugly. At issue was whether the US Forest Service should repair the road, which provided the only vehicle access into the Jarbidge Wilderness Area. But repairing the road might damage water quality in Jarbidge Creek, thereby threatening an endangered fish. Instead, the Forest Service decided to close the road. That decision angered local residents, many of whom viewed the Service's conclusion as another example of an overbearing federal government telling them what to do with their land. Although the county claimed it owned the road, people still sent 10,000 shovels to the courthouse in protest and rented bulldozers and other equipment to rebuild the road themselves. The local forest ranger's office was even firebombed.

Federal Mediation

"It was a highly controversial issue," notes an understated Kirk Emerson, director of the Tucson, Arizona–based US Institute for Environmental Conflict Resolution. The federal district court in Nevada asked the US Institute to help resolve the dispute. Emerson and her staff researched the various positions, negotiated with all sides on the conditions for negotiations, made the administrative arrangements, and assisted the parties in selecting a mediator. In the end, after several court appearances, political wrangling, and further intense negotiations, the Forest Service agreed to recognize county ownership of the road, and the county promised to comply fully with environmental laws in repairing and maintaining it.

"We provide a fair and balanced context for arriving at real agreements that can be implemented," Emerson says of the US Institute's role in mediating environmental disputes like the one in Nevada. "We offer a thoughtful, new approach to solving environmental problems. We can help bring parties to the negotiating table and help them see each other's viewpoints. Getting them there is 80 percent of the work."

Environmental Conflict Resolution

Although not everyone uses it yet, government agencies, private-sector companies, environmental groups, landowners, and individuals are increasingly turning to environmental conflict resolution [ECR]. Consensus-building techniques are used to address issues that previously were often subjected to lengthy and contentious political, legal, or public relations campaigns. "We were seeing [environmental] issue after issue come before us and create gridlock in Congress and the courts," says Senator John McCain (R-AZ), sponsor of the 1998 law that created the US Institute. "There had to be a better way to resolve these problems."

Environmental conflict resolution represents that better way, says Eleanor Winsor, president of Winsor Associates, a Washington, DC, mediation firm. The process "provides a forum where people can come together and help shape a project," Winsor says. "When it works, [conflict resolution] can help achieve a better project with less opposition because it takes people's needs into consideration. It is a very powerful democratic force."

Consensus-building approaches can be applied to disputes over where to put electric transmission lines, power plants, or wastewater treatment facilities, for example, says Lawrence Susskind, professor of urban and environmental planning at the Massachusetts Institute of Technology [MIT] and director of the MIT-Harvard Public Disputes Program. These approaches, used for local, regional, or even national issues, can generate agreements that could later be enacted into law or accepted by the courts. Dispute resolution cannot replace the political process, Susskind says, but it can supplement it.

Environmental conflict resolution works best, Winsor states, when parties to a dispute recognize that compromise may work better not only for them but for the public as well. It also works best when the costs of mediation are divided among the parties, rather than being the sole responsibility of one. And it works best when the mediator, facilitator, or other third-party convener is recognized by all parties as impartial and independent. "Mediation can help very alienated and polarized parties find common ground rather than demonizing each other," says John Bickerman, a Washington, DC, lawyer and founder of Bickerman Dispute Resolution.

Problems with ECR

On the other hand, conflict resolution is not always the chosen means of resolving environmental, land use, or natural resource issues. Some parties to a dispute may use mediation or negotiations for what Winsor calls "a front" for behind-the-scenes political and legal maneuvering or to win public support for their position. One party may want to set a legal precedent, something a negotiated compromise cannot achieve. In fact, conflict resolution is unlikely to work when one party feels it can win a legal, political, or public relations victory and thus sees no reason to compromise.

Furthermore, negotiating values is more difficult than negotiating interests. "Wolf control of any kind won't satisfy people who believe wolves have a right to be there," says Christopher Moore, a partner and conflict-management specialist at CDR Associates, a Boulder, Colorado, firm. Moreover, negotiation may be difficult if not impossible when one party views the other as the enemy and compromise as a sellout. In other words, Emerson says, environmental conflict resolution "is no panacea."

Although no one knows when conflict resolution was first used in environmental disputes, the practice became widespread in the 1980s, Susskind says. It was institutionalized in 1990 when Congress passed the Administrative Dispute Resolution and the Regulatory Negotiation Acts. The two laws were combined in a 1996 reauthorization that required all US government departments and agencies to appoint an alternative dispute resolution official and to adopt policies for implementing the process internally.

U.S. Institute

During the same period, Susskind adds, some two-dozen states created environmental dispute resolution offices. There are now several hundred full-time mediators, negotiators, facilitators, and other professionals engaged in environmental conflict resolution, most of whom are working within nonprofit companies, law firms, and universities. As many as a thousand others may do at least some conflict resolution work. The US Institute for Environmental Conflict Resolution maintains a national roster of nearly 200 professional mediators that anyone can use to find an impartial negotiator.

The US Institute itself operates as a federal program within the Morris K. Udall Scholarship and Excellence in National Environmental Policy Foundation. The Udall Foundation is one of five congressionally chartered foundations, which are part of the federal government but are independent of each other and other US government departments and agencies. The Udall Foundation seeks to foster a greater understanding of the environment, public lands and natural resources, and Native American affairs. It does so mostly through undergraduate scholarships, doctoral fellowships, and internships, for Native American students.

By law, the US Institute seeks to resolve environmental disputes involving a federal agency (or any environmental and natural resource issue of national concern), increase the appropriate use of environmental conflict resolution as a technique for mediating disputes, and reduce the number of disputes by developing a process for building consensus for solving problems during the early stages of environmental decisionmaking. Priority is given to disputes involving more than one federal agency, especially where there is a conflict between agencies, and to problems touching on highly technical or scientific issues.

Since January 1999, the US Institute has handled more than 100 cases in 30 states and the District of Columbia. Usually, the institute suggests the names of professional mediators or facilitators listed on its national roster. In some cases, institute staff have helped parties develop processes for reaching agreement without outside mediation. In other disputes, it helped bring stakeholders and government officials together in ways that allowed all sides to recognize each other's viewpoints and legal constraints. Most often, the US Institute becomes involved in environmental disputes at the request of a government agency or federal judge.

Take the case of issues surrounding bison and elk herds in northwestern Wyoming. The US Fish and Wildlife Service, National Park Service, Forest Service, and the Wyoming Game and Fish Department were preparing to adopt management plans for the herds in the Yellowstone and Grand Teton National Parks, National Elk Refuge, and Bridger-Teton National Forest. Before doing so, the agencies asked the US Institute in 1999 to conduct a situation assessment to help them design ways to involve the public in the planning process. A situation assessment is used to identify solutions to issues without going through formal mediation or negotiation.

Yellowstone Controversy

Bison and elk management in the Greater Yellowstone area has become controversial because the wild animals carry brucellosis, a disease that can be transmitted to cattle, causing pregnant cows to abort. Ranchers outside the national parks, forests, and wilderness areas have shot affected bison that wander onto private or state lands. Animal rights groups opposed the killings. When a court ordered the federal government to undertake a second and more comprehensive environmental impact statement, the Department of the Interior asked the US Institute to address the issues.

An assessment team composed of members from the US Institute, the University of Wyoming, and the Denver, Colorado–based Meridian Institute attended agency and other meetings, identified the range of issues and affected interests, and sought comments from all stakeholders. The team identified goals shared by ranchers, environmentalists, and others interested in the issue. These included, Emerson says, a vision of healthy wild herds, a recognition of the animals' national significance, a change in how the agencies manage the herds and deal with one another, and a need for more scientific information on which to base management plans. Consequently, the institute and its partners recommended that the public have direct input in planning for the herds' management, greater access to technical information, the opportunity to interact with the scientists, and representation on planning groups studying alternative management plans.

The Tucson Rod and Gun Club

Meanwhile, a continuing dispute has engaged the US Institute closer to home. The dispute involves a target range run by the Tucson Rod and Gun Club within Sabino Canyon Recreation Area, a part of Coronado National Forest in the Santa Catalina Mountains. Sabino Canyon is one of the most popular Sonoran Desert sites for tourists and locals alike in Arizona.

The Benefits of Environmental Conflict Resolution

We will see healthy environments and communities. More powerful and healthy environments in which to build on and live in. Our community will be happy and productive. Our families will be strong and our environments will be on the road to restoration.

The community sees there is a healthy way of dealing with conflict and 100% consensus can be achieved. Conflicts are resolved. Consensus is reached.

Bob Chadwzck, "Beyond Conflict to Consensus,"
Managing Wholes: Creating a Future that Works,
September 2002. http://managingwholes.com/conflict1.htm.

The US Forest Service suspended shooting at the club's half-century-old target range in 1997 because of safety and compatibility concerns, much to the delight of many nearby homeowners, hikers, and environmentalists. In response, the gun club and its supporters appealed the Forest Service's decision, filed a lawsuit, and enlisted the aid of the Arizona congressional delegation and state legislators, actions that could have mired the issue in controversy for years.

The Forest Service asked the US Institute to act as an impartial, outside mediator to help resolve the dispute. At issue, were, and still are, questions about noise, hazardous materials, and whether a gun range should continue to be located in what is now a populated area. After more than a year of negotiations, the gun club agreed to submit proposals to clean up and contain all bullets within the range, but the Forest Service rejected them as inadequate. The gun club submitted new proposals last fall, but most of those have been rejected too.

Although the controversy has receded, the future of the range remains uncertain, says John McGee, supervisor of Coronado National Forest.

ECR and Environmental Disputes

Not all environmental disputes have involved the US Institute. In one case that generated significant controversy and head-lines, CDR Associates was asked to help mediate a dispute over use of water from the American and Sacramento Rivers in California. The issues, say CDR's Christopher Moore, are whether, how much, from which sites, and at what times of the year the East Bay Municipal Utility District (EBMUD) could take water from the American River for use in the Oak-land area. The American flows west from the Sierra Nevada Mountains in eastern California to the city of Sacramento, where it joins the Sacramento River on its way to San Fran-cisco Bay.

The city and county, governments of Sacramento as well as local environmentalists opposed plans to take water from the American River. They argued that lower water levels would reduce recreational opportunities, harm salmon runs, and cause the river to run dry during droughts. EBMUD said its choices were limited by water quality standards issued by the US Environmental Protection Agency under the Clean Water Act.

After nearly a decade of legal and political wrangling, Moore worked out a compromise whereby EBMUD would abandon plans to take American River water. Instead, the util-ity would get water from the Sacramento River just a few miles downstream from where the American joined it. Earlier, the utility had dismissed that alternative because EPA [Envi-ronmental Protection Agency] water quality standards re-quired it to treat Sacramento but not American River water. Now, though, new EPA standards required the utility to treat water from both rivers alike. Although the original lawsuits were dismissed following the agreement, the issue may not be completely resolved. Some local environmentalists have raised questions about the effects of taking water from the Sacramento River. "We may wind up back in negotiation," Moore says.

Elsewhere, some 1650 miles to the southeast, similar issues have drawn mediators into a dispute involving the Edwards-Trinity aquifer, the primary source of municipal water in the San Antonio, Texas, area. John Fleming, deputy director of the Center for Public Policy Dispute Resolution at the University of Texas School of Law in Austin, was asked by the US Geological Survey [USGS] in 2000 to help facilitate its research plans. USGS undertakes geological and environmental research that, among other things, could affect how much, where, and for what purposes water is taken from the Edwards-Trinity aquifer.

At issue, Fleming says, were competing municipal and agricultural uses of the aquifer's water, Increased use of the aquifer could lower water levels. That, in turn, could dry out natural springs and threaten the existence of animals that live in them, including several species of rare and endangered salamanders. Fleming headed a team of facilitators who worked with USGS to convene stakeholder meetings to help the agency identify research projects. Built into the process were opportunities to resolve potential conflicts through negotiation before they became lawsuits. "We think this can be a model for other agencies," he says.

Whether and to what extent these kinds of mediations, negotiations, and facilitations help resolve environmental disputes and keep more of them out of the political and court systems remains to be seen. For his part, Senator McCain remains cautious. "It's too soon to tell," he says. The US Institute for Environmental Conflict Resolution's Emerson, on the other hand, is confident these approaches will help. She argues that society now recognizes how complex natural systems are and that competing interests need to come together to protect them. That requires more careful and thoughtful approaches to reaching consensus-based solutions to disputes.

The "Ebb and Flow" of ECR

At least some others agree. Conflict resolution represents "the cusp of some real innovative ways to resolve some of the thorniest environmental problems," says Robert Cunningham, the Forest Service's assistant director of planning. "We get 400–500 lawsuits a year. Environmental conflict resolution lets us make wiser choices on natural resources in a more rational way. We can do environmental planning without the different interests at war with each other. We can work together to reach agreements."

A consensus-based approach to resolving disputes is "a better way of getting things done," adds William Hall, the US Environmental Protection Agency's conflict resolution specialist. The process allows EPA and other government agencies to reach better environmental decisions faster, at lower cost, and with more durable results, because the affected interests and general public are part of the decisionmaking process, Hall says.

That may be so. But CDR's Moore compares environmental conflict resolution with the ebb and flow of the ocean tides on the shore. It all depends, he says, on what administration is in office and who heads individual government agencies. For her part, Emerson hopes the practice is building momentum. "People are beginning to see the positive results of two decades of environmental mediation," she says. "We can build relationships between government agencies and landowners. We can get people to talk to each other. We can help resolve conflicting authorities, mandates, and missions."

❙ *"The use of [environmental conflict resolution] . . . invokes a trade-off."*

Environmental Conflict Resolution Has Benefits but Remains Untested

E. Franklin Dukes

The following viewpoint examines whether environmental conflict resolution (ECR) is an effective means of alternative dispute resolution (ADR). The author contends that not enough research has been done to declare ECR a success. For instance, many disputes that use ECR still resort to traditional legal action. Furthermore, ECR sometimes results in a loss of legitimacy of mediated settlements because of the secrecy often involved in negotiations. E. Franklin Dukes is the director of the University of Virginia's Institute for Environmental Negotiation.

As you read, consider the following questions:

1. According to the viewpoint, environmental conflict is a subset of what larger category of strife?
2. Besides mediation, what are the other types of environmental conflict resolution, as stated by the author?

E. Franklin Dukes, "What We Know About Environmental Conflict Resolution," *Conflict Resolution Quarterly*, vol. 22, 2004, pp. 191–220. Copyright © 2004 Wiley Periodicals, Inc. and the Association for Conflict Resolution. Reprinted with permission of John Wiley & Sons, Inc.

3. What are the "traditional procedures" of ECR as described in the viewpoint?

Environmental conflicts typically involve many different types of parties, issues, and resources. Such conflicts may occur upstream over policy, which means laws or regulations about how a particular issue or class of issues will be addressed, or downstream about place, which refers to what has occurred or will occur in a particular circumstance.

Environmental Disputes

Practically every community finds itself embroiled in periodic disputes over public land use and preservation, private land development, water quality or quantity, air quality, habitat for species, waste disposal, natural resource use and management, environmental hazards, and more. What is often at stake in such conflicts are fundamental issues: individual and community health, racial and ethnic justice, the survival or death of entire species, the integrity or destruction of whole ecosystems, and the economic or cultural viability of various human communities.

Environmental conflict is a subset of the larger category of public conflicts involving issues such as health and health care, race and ethnicity, economic development, and governance. Environmental conflict often includes some combination of these issues. It also may involve multiple jurisdictions and multiple levels of jurisdictions (international, federal, tribal, regional, state, and local), and the conflict may be less about the resources at stake than about issues of jurisdiction or precedent.

Early research and theory building in the environmental conflict resolution arena focused on mediation. The vocabulary that at one point favored *mediation* has expanded to include terms such as *consensus building, collaboration, collaborative learning, collaborative planning, collaborative natural resource management, community-based collaboration,* and *community-based conservation.* Many practitioners would include *enhanced public involvement* within their practice as well. Some work encompasses a combination of such processes.

For this article, *environmental conflict resolution* (ECR) serves as an umbrella term for this entire range of processes. The characteristics that identify an ECR process include direct, face-to-face discussions; deliberation intended to enhance participants' mutual education and understanding; inclusion of multiple sectors representing diverse and often conflicting perspectives; openness and flexibility of process; and consensus or some variation other than unilateral decision making as the basis for agreements. ECR may or may not include a third-party mediator or facilitator. The subject matter includes some environmental element, by which is meant the interconnected biophysical, economic, political, and social systems encompassing both natural and human systems. . . .

Research and Environmental Conflict Resolution

Perhaps the most compelling question is how ECR compares to other ways of addressing environmental conflicts. Analysts of ECR, proponents and critics alike, commonly think of it as an alternative to other processes. These so-called traditional procedures include primarily legislation, administrative decision making (agency rules and regulations), and adjudication.

There are times when that distinction makes sense. But the risk is that we fail to appreciate that ECR processes are less often alternatives and more often one part of a complex and interdependent system of legal, legislative, or administrative processes.

Many environmental conflicts, and all complex and enduring ones, play themselves out in a number of forums involv-

The Limits of Alternative Dispute Resolution

Even its most ardent supporters ... reluctantly admit that ADR [alternative dispute resolution] is not a miracle cure-all for the deficiencies of traditional dispute resolution processes. Most would agree that the following are legitimate statements regarding the limitations of ADR:

- ADR does not eliminate conflict; it is a way of addressing it. Nor is ADR necessarily non-adversarial;

- ADR cannot guarantee a resolution of all disputes. Fundamental differences in values, for example, are not amenable to compromise;

- ADR cannot achieve all desired outcomes; for example, it cannot establish a legal precedent; and

- ADR works best in circumstances where (a) an articulated dispute exists, (b) there are a small number of readily identifiable parties, (c) the issues between the parties are clear, (d) the parties are willing to compromise and (e) the parties have control over or can influence decision making.

Elizabeth Swanson,
"Environmental Conflict: Is ADR the Solution?"
LawNow, April–May 1997, pp. 15–18.

ing a variety of processes. ECR influences and in turn is influenced by these other processes. . . .

Furthermore, the conflict behavior that some want to resolve is exactly the conflict behavior that others want to see. That is, the preferred alternative to ECR may actually be continuation or even escalation of the conflict. This is certainly true of some critics of ECR for whom the term *collaboration* or *mediation* too often equates with selling short the environment.

Settlement Rates

Is there any way of gauging what proportion of cases handled by ECR processes reach agreement, and can that rate be compared in any meaningful way to non-ECR processes? Does that rate in fact mean anything?. . .

The pilot mediation program in the U.S. District Court for the District of Oregon . . . is telling. Seventy-five environmental cases "not easily resolved by a judicial decision or by a traditional evaluative settlement conference" were screened for potential mediation during the pilot. Thirteen proceeded to mediation; seven were essentially distributive in nature, mostly involving cleanup costs. Of these seven, only two were resolved during mediation. One case was still under negotiation but likely to settle without a return to mediation. Two of the seven returned to litigation; one of those had used a settlement judge rather than an external mediator. One returned to litigation to address a single issue and then returned to mediation to work out an arbitration process. One went to mediation but paired the mediator with an expert adviser; the parties returned to further discovery even as mediation remained an option at the time the pilot ended. Of the six complex integrative cases that proceeded to mediation, three settled and one withdrew before agreeing on a mediator. One case was still pending, and one did not settle despite resolution of the major issues because "a dispute over attorney fees remained". Finally, twenty-three of the seventy-five reviewed cases that did not proceed to mediation settled before trial. One of the remaining cases was settled in a mediation conducted outside the pilot program, and one case that involved a former mediation participant reported using a similar process to reach settlement. Two cases settled using a settlement judge. That left thirty-six cases continuing in litigation as the study ended.

This study illustrates the difficulty of isolating ECR from other processes. And this is the case in an environment circumscribed by the judicial system, whereas much, if not most, ECR work occurs outside the courts (no research delineates how much ECR work occurs and where)....

[T.C.] Beirle and [J.] Cayford place consensus-seeking dispute resolution at one end of a continuum of methods for engaging the public in environmental decision making. At the other end are informal consultations. And in the middle would be ranged familiar processes such as public hearings, meetings, workshops, visioning exercises, and design charrettes [workshops]. What do we know about any differences between and among these processes ranged along this continuum?

Beirle and Cayford examined 239 cases of environmental decision making on the basis of five key goals of public participation: (1) incorporating public values, (2) improving decision quality, (3) resolving conflict, (4) building institutional trust, and (5) educating the public. They unambiguously declare that dispute resolution has been "clearly more effective in achieving the social goals of public participation". But they offer a large caveat: these goals are achieved "... only among the small group of participants". They are "much less effective" in using outreach to spread the benefits of education and trust formation beyond the group.

They conclude that agreement-focused ECR processes "limit whose values are heard, whose conflicts are resolved, and whose priority issues are addressed". The use of ECR invokes a trade-off of "success and significance". Most important for program managers and convenors of such processes, the loss in legitimacy among a wider public sometimes means that agreements are revisited or rejected when other actors get involved.

This finding prompts an important question: How is agreement valued relative to other potential ECR outcomes? This question has prompted scrutiny for many years. [The scholar S.A. Moore] developed a rubric for evaluating outcomes directly from participants' views of success. Although derived from a limited database of two case studies involving long-term planning efforts on public lands in Australia and the United States, her analysis reveals the many ways participants themselves define and evaluate success. She introduces the concept of conditional success, where judgment is withheld until there is evidence of implementation or durability. Moore suggests that participants think of success within four dimensions: political, interests, responsibility, and relationship. Politically oriented success refers to acceptance by interested communities such that implementation was politically feasible. Interest-oriented success means protection and enhancement of participant interests. Responsibility-oriented success means the extent that participants feel continuing ownership in the product. The fourth dimension, relationship-oriented success, reflects the quality of relationships among and between factions, public agencies, and the broader community. Participants consider both process and outcome when judging success, and more than half of the sixty-six interviewees in her study referred to more than one dimension when describing success. [S]he notes that mediations judged unsuccessful by a mediator may in fact be considered successful by participants.

[J.] Innes has published much of her research in planning journals. In the most thorough and weightiest tome the field of ECR has yet produced, *The Consensus Building Handbook*, Innes, offers the results of years of studying ECR and in particular long-term collaborative groups addressing environmental issues. She . . . explains not only why outcomes other than agreement are important but which outcomes are important and how collaborative processes can achieve those outcomes.

I have argued elsewhere that an ideology of management—whereby public decision making (whether in law, planning, public administration, or ECR) focuses on improved efficiency, productivity and managerial capability of authorities—competes with a vision of conflict transformation. The most valued outcomes of ECR are not necessarily settlements, however important those may be (and in most circumstances where agreement is sought they are likely to be important). Instead, in many cases, the relational by-products are exactly the outcomes most appreciated by participants. Innes provides the most comprehensive articulation of how the ECR process can lead to specific transformative outcomes.

| "*Conflict resolution techniques have grown in importance as water managers increasingly are called upon to resolve conflicts.*"

Conflict Resolution Strategies Ease Resource Conflicts

Faye Anderson

In the following viewpoint, Faye Anderson examines the causes of conflicts over water resources, especially the nature and sources of conflict, including conflicting goals, factual disagreements and distrust, and power struggles. The viewpoint contends that resource conflicts were often seen in the past as "technical" issues that could be solved by science or innovation, but increasingly, conflict resolution techniques are the preferred method to resolve disputes. Faye Anderson works at the American Water Resources Association and is an author who writes frequently on resource issues.

As you read, consider the following questions:

1. According to the viewpoint, what kind of resource is water?

2. What countries cited in the viewpoint are experiencing conflicts over dam-building?

3. According to the author, what three factors lead to factual disagreements?

Water resources management increasingly requires compromise and consensus if solutions to problems are to be formulated and implement ed. As issues of competing uses intensify, water decisionmakers are increasingly called upon to manage people as well as the water resource itself.

The Nature of Conflict

Conflict can be defined as disagreement over the appropriate course of action to be taken in a particular situation. Conflict abounds as individuals and groups have different values, priorities, interests, and hopes for the future. Conflicts take place between neighbors, communities, states, regions, and nations. Areas of severe water conflict correlate with water scarcity; hence, the regions with the greatest conflict and potential for conflict are the Middle East, the Indian subcontinent, and the former Soviet Union.

Water is a fugitive resource. As water moves through the hydrologic cycle [the natural process in which water circulates through rain and evaporation], it does not pay any attention to political boundaries and conflicts that often result between differing political units. These types of conflicts are referred to as transboundary water issues. Conflicts also arise between different groups in society, such as business interests and environmental groups, or between parties located upstream and downstream.

The ultimate conflict is armed conflict. Many fears have been expressed that water wars will occur in the future as water becomes more and more scarce. Historical studies have not supported this hypothesis that water disputes lead to war. There are only a couple of documented situations in all of history where war broke out over water. Although most water conflicts are nonviolent, they still have serious implications for societal welfare.

Sources of Conflict: Conflicting Goals

Conflict can result from many factors. The sources of conflicts must be understood in order to manage water resources effectively. Three basic sources of conflict are conflicting goals, factual disagreements, and ineffective relationships (distrust and power struggles).

Water planning and management activities are undertaken for the purpose of solving problems such as inadequate water supplies or poor water quality. For water planning efforts to be undertaken, the problem to be solved must be clearly identified and understood. Once a problem is identified, possible courses of action to address the problem can be enumerated and then the best course of action can be chosen and implemented.

In reality, however, the preferred course of action to solve a problem depends on goals, values, and objectives. Goals are statements of a desired future situation, where stated goals then function as criteria for evaluating alternative courses of action. Thus, the process of goal-setting actually serves to influence the ultimate actions taken to achieve these goals. Goals are related to the decision-making participants' interests and values.

Conflicting goals are common in water management scenarios. For example, dam-building is controversial around the world. Several large dam projects have engendered conflict with local peoples over the best ways to provide water supplies, protect the environment, and the rights of relocated groups to their homes. These conflicts are local, but have also attracted international attention from environmental and human rights groups. These groups work together in order to influence the local government to stop building the dam, and

Water Conflicts Must Be Addressed

One critical aim of water management is to continually reconcile opposing interests of all water users—be they individuals, enterprises, corporations, interest groups, administrative or sovereign entities. The management of water conflicts, confrontations, competitions and co-operation are thus a part of water resources management in its broadest sense. Negative interactions (such as competition and confrontations) over scarce water resources can lead to tension and—in extreme situations—even conflict, should they remain unattended.

United Nation's Educational, Scientific and Cultural Organization (UNESCO), "Potentional Conflict to Cooperation Potential (PCCP): Mission Statement."
www.unesco.org/water/wwap/pccp.

to persuade the banks to eliminate loan money to fund the dam. These types of conflicts over dam-building are currently seen in India, Turkey, China, and many other countries needing to meet the rising water demands of their large populations.

The clashing desires to achieve different goals lead to much conflict in the water management process. In the example above, the conflict is between the goals of water supply and hydropower versus the goals of social and environmental preservation. In such instances, it is difficult to resolve conflicting goals. In these cases, the parties may agree on the effects of certain actions but disagree on the desirability of these effects, and therefore fundamentally disagree on the desirability of the action itself. Thus, goal-setting is an important water management activity requiring the participation of all relevant stakeholders.

Factual Disagreements

Sometimes, differences over the preferred course of action to solve water problems stem from disagreements over the facts, or perceived facts, of the situation. These disagreements are often genuine differences of opinion, and can be related to the poor quality of information or to a lack of data. For example, in the previous example of dam-building, factual disagreements may arise over the exact sediment load of the river, the actual need for additional water supplies, the ability to finance the project, or the legal rights the local people have according to national laws. In practice, facts are rarely clear-cut pieces of information; on the contrary, they often are infused with information stemming from individual or group values and interests.

Several factors can lead to factual disagreements. First, facts are rarely completely certain and their degree of uncertainty can influence how much conflict may result. This uncertainty exists because human knowledge is incomplete or imperfect. Furthermore, there are limitations to science and scientific methods. For example, people may not completely understand how contaminants travel through a specific groundwater system, nor how water is actually used in a given locality. Often assumptions are substituted for agreed-upon facts. This lack of information constrains decision-making processes and opens up room for parties to debate the facts utilized in decision-making.

Second, factual disagreements can stem from the situation in which the parties have different information. Many times, parties rely on completely different sets of information for their decision-making, and may not share or discuss the information with the conflicting party. For example, hydropower providers tend to look at the quantity, cost, and profit level of power to potentially be generated. Yet local environmental groups tend to look at the state of water systems, and threats to those systems. Each group has its own network from which they collect information. Sometimes groups may even exaggerate factual disagreements to achieve their own desired goals in the decision-making process.

Third, factual disagreements can arise from limitations of parties' abilities to process information. Many water management problems are very complex. Psychological research often shows that both the expert and average citizen can use only a few pieces of information when drawing conclusions in decision-making. Which pieces are actually used and the weight attached to them differs widely from individual to individual. And sometimes, people are not consistent in decision-making. All these factors help explain many seemingly factual disagreements between parties in water management processes.

Distrust and Power Struggles

The third source of conflict stems from the state of the ongoing relationship between the disagreeing parties, particularly issues of distrust and power struggles. A situation of distrust breeds conflict, as parties have no foundation for communication and collaborative problem-solving activities. Distrust is often the result of poor communication and can often lead to further misunderstandings. These tensions often cause parties to be less willing or even unwilling to cooperate with each other. Sometimes distrust is the result of personality conflicts or historical circumstances.

Power struggles are related to distrust and take the form of competition over various sources of power related to the decision-making process, such as financial resources, access to the media, and access to information. Parties are struggling for power rather than attending to solving the water problem at hand.

It is difficult to resolve power struggles, and parties often find themselves locked into these types of conflicts. Sometimes these parties will refuse to accept workable solutions because the power struggle becomes more important than solving the actual problem, and they might be perceived as weak for accepting a compromise. These relationship-based factors among the stakeholders can generate conflict in water management scenarios.

Conflict Resolution

More than one source of conflict may be present in any water management situation. Due to these prevalent sources of conflict, conflict resolution is an essential component of current water management activities around the world. Many conflicts are taken to court systems where they can be costly to resolve, in terms of both time and money. Some disputes are repeatedly taken to the courts and thus are never truly resolved.

Resolving conflict requires compromise. And compromise often involves (1) a willingness to accept the validity of another party to hold a different perspective; (2) an attempt to understand other perspectives even when those perspectives are not accepted; and (3) a search for solutions that will accommodate diverse interests.

In the past, water management issues were often viewed as technical problems that could be "cured" by structural solutions such as reservoirs, dams, and levees. Satisfying water demands was the primary goal.

But today, water resources are increasingly scarce, populations have grown, and water management is much more complex. Financial considerations have grown in importance, given society's tight budgets and the major expenses of water-related infrastructure. Environmental considerations are more prominent with greater societal awareness and concern for detrimental impacts to the environment.

All of these factors have increased the potential for conflict in water management activities. Hence, conflict resolution techniques have grown in importance as water managers increasingly are called upon to resolve conflicts.

Methods that water managers can use to resolve specific types of conflict include the following.

Conflicting Goals

- Developing a common vision of the future among stakeholders

- Educating stakeholders and conducting public awareness activities

- Finding win-win solutions

- Compensating those who will experience losses stemming from a solution

- Promoting holistic understandings of water problems

Factual Disagreements

- Promoting effective communication over areas of genuine disagreement

- Undertaking additional research to generate better data

- Promoting joint research or research performed by the third party

Distrust and Power Struggles

- Developing better relationships between the parties

- Taking parties out of their familiar environments

- Getting parties to listen to each other

- Finding common ground or self-interests

- Bringing in a mediator

These types of solutions can be valuable in resolving conflict and promoting effective long-term answers to water problems. Conflict is not necessarily a bad or undesirable thing, and it often presents an opportunity for much-needed dialogue. Conflict can also help identify where things need to be done better.

The challenge for water managers is to ensure that conflict is a constructive force in decision-making processes and that it does not become destructive. Ignoring conflict can lead to greater conflict in the future and thus impairs the implementation of potential solutions to water-related problems. Water managers must effectively deal with conflict if water management is to be successful and benefit society.

> *"Division and distribution of a static resource is difficult enough, but problems are magnified when the resource is able to flow across international boundaries."*

Sometimes Countries Resort to Military Intervention Because of Resource Conflicts

Isabelle Humphries

In the viewpoint that follows, the author traces the basis of the ongoing Arab-Israeli conflict to disputes over control of water. The viewpoint contends that groups in the region are willing to go to war over resources such as water and that these international mediation efforts have failed to end conflict. It also asserts that Israel continues to violate international agreements by taking far more than its share of water from disputed territories. Isabelle Humphries is a scholar who researches the Palestinian refugee community in Israel.

Isabelle Humphries, "Breaching Borders: The Role of Water in the Middle East Conflict," *Washington Report on Middle East Affairs*, September/October 2006, pp. 20–21. www.wrmea.com/archives/Sept_Oct_2006/0609020.html. Copyright © 2006 American Educational Trust. All rights reserved. Reproduced by permission.

As you read, consider the following questions:

1. According to the viewpoint, what started the 1967 war?
2. Under the terms of the 1993 Oslo Accord, as stated in the viewpoint, what four groups of people are supposed to share the Jordan River?
3. How long did the United Nations estimate it would be before Palestinians in the Gaza territory run out of drinkable water, according to the author?

In months when Israel is not pounding the life out of its Lebanese neighbors, a tourist to Israel may hire a car and drive around the beautiful northern regions of former mandate Palestine and Syria. Here one may look around at the stunningly green surroundings, go kayaking in the Jordan River, admire the beautiful waterfalls at ancient Banyas in the Golan, or dip one's feet in the waters of the Sea of Galilee. Those feeling adventurous may hand over their passports at the gate, enter the Israeli-occupied Alawite village of Ghajar, and look down at the little stream of the Wazzani in the small valley below.

Israel has not ensconced itself in the Golan Heights for mere tourism opportunities, however. The Israeli media machine would have one believe that the country is engaged in a struggle to protect its very existence against imaginary Arab military giants. Yet a trip around the places in which it chooses to maintain its borders is far more revealing of the root of conflict with its Arab neighbors—water. Israel has no plans to make peace with Syria and return the Golan Heights, because by doing so it would give up its control of springs, rivers and the Sea of Galilee. Nor will it hand over any significant West Bank land to Palestinians, for in doing so Israel would have to abandon lush aquifers (underground water reserves), key access to the Dead Sea, the Jordan River, and surrounding fertile plains.

Control of Water

Division and distribution of a static resource such as land is difficult enough, but problems are magnified when the resource is able to flow across international boundaries. Take the Israeli furor over Lebanon's installation of new pumping facilities on the Wazzani River in the fall of 2002. Despite the fact that the activity took place entirely on Lebanese land, Israel raised a ruckus because the Wazzani is a key tributary of the Hasbani River. And although the Hasbani flows for 25 miles inside Lebanon, it crosses into the Israeli-occupied Syrian Golan, feeding into the Banias and Dan Rivers, which in turn flow into the Jordan—ultimately providing water to the rapidly reducing Sea of Galilee, Israel's largest source of fresh water.

While Beirut stated that it was Lebanon's internationally recognized right to pump Wazzani waters for surrounding low-income Shi'i villages, Israel objected, claiming, as usual, that the "terrorist" entities of Syria and Hezbollah were behind the development plan. Lebanon retorted by pointing out that, even after pump installation, it would be taking only 10 million cubic meters annually—while Israel, on the other hand, uses some 150 million cubic meters a year from the Wazzani and Hasbani.

That particular episode of the water conflict did not erupt into full-scale war, but at other times water has provided the trigger. In his memoirs, [former Israeli prime minister] Ariel Sharon claimed that the 1967 war (resulting in Israeli occupation of the Golan and prevention of Syrian access to the Sea of Galilee) was launched as an unavoidable response to Syrian attempts three years earlier to divert the headwaters of the Jordan.

The Historical Evidence

An analysis of historical evidence, however, provides a very different story of the events leading to the 1967 war. It was Is-

Water and Conflict

On the International level, tensions between countries that share a river basin may hinder sustainable development—thus indirectly driving poverty, migration and social instability. They also have the potential to exacerbate other non-water-related violent conflicts.

Development Assistance Committee,
"Water and Violent Conflict,"
Mainstreaming Conflict Resolution.
www.globalpolicy.org/security/natres
/water/2005/052605waterconflict.pdf.

rael, in fact, which first made moves to divert the headwaters, provoking an international crisis, yet convincing many that Syria was the aggressor. Israeli historian Avi Shlaim dates Israel's first attempt to divert the Jordan River to as early as 1953, when Syria responded not by attacking the Jewish state, but complaining to the U.N. [United Nations], which eventually put a halt to the Israeli plan the following year. Ten years later, however, Israel began to pump water from the Sea of Galilee into its National Water Carrier—a grave threat to vital Syrian, Lebanese and Jordanian water sources. It was in response to this Israeli move that Syria planned to divert Jordan water into its own territory.

Remaining in control of the Golan Heights today allows Israel to irrigate settlements as far as the Negev desert through its National Water Carrier pipeline. The diversion of waters to this artificial carrier has grave implications, resulting in the depletion and salinization of the Jordan River south of the Sea of Galilee, and devastating agriculture on the Jordanian side of the river. The Jordanian government's diversion of the Yarmuk cannot adequately compensate for this loss.

Israeli control of water is as much of a concern for Palestinians as it is for Arab neighbors. Whether for the few Palestinian farmers remaining inside the Israeli state, or those in the West Bank and Gaza, Israeli water policy is directed at destroying any remaining Palestinian agriculture.... Even where Palestinians remain in control of small pieces of land, Israeli water policy usually sees to it that there is not enough water to grow crops.

Situated above the mountain aquifer, central West Bank towns such as Qalqilya and Nablus have traditionally exported crops across the Middle East. Yet today, despite the availability of sophisticated technology, Israeli policy means that many Palestinians do not have enough water even for themselves, let alone to irrigate the few fields that have not yet been confiscated.

Oslo Accords

Palestinians should have ready access to water from the mountain aquifer (divided into three), the Jordan River basin and the Gazan coastal aquifer. Aquifers are replenished through rainwater seeping through the ground, and water accessible via wells and springs. According to Oslo [a 1993 accord between Israel and Palestine], two West Bank aquifers are to be shared between Israelis and Palestinians, leaving the Gazan coastal and the third West Bank aquifer solely to Palestinians. (Palestinians, of course, have no access to the Sea of Galilee— their share having been taken in 1948.) According to Oslo, Syrians, Jordanians, Palestinians and Israelis all have a share in the Jordan River system (although 97 percent of the river passes through areas only occupied by Israel since 1967). Currently Israel has assured that its citizens have the highest per capita water consumption in the entire Middle East—and four times as much as the Palestinians among whom they live.

International law clearly states that Israel should not be taking water from areas occupied in 1967. Yet even if Oslo had been followed to the letter, it assured inequality by giving Israeli water authorities overall control of water resources. Palestinians may not drill for water without Israeli approval, yet Israel can pump as much water as it likes into its illegal settlements. More than 80 percent of West Bank water is taken by Israelis on both sides of the 1967 line.

Israeli occupation has prevented the development of a Palestinian water infrastructure which would make maximum use of the minimum resources. Some 200,000 West Bankers do not even have access to piped water systems, while the settlements around them are kept green with lawn sprinklers. Palestinians living under occupation are forced to rely on expensive private water tankers, which of course cannot reach them in times of closure. Ironically, some of the water is bought directly from Israelis at inflated prices, despite the fact that the water originates in the West Bank.

Israeli Violations of Agreements

In contravention of Oslo, Israel continues to pump from the Gaza coastal aquifer—which, as levels fall dangerously low, draws in salt water from the Mediterranean. Two-thirds of water is used for the Israeli agricultural sector, which represents only 3 percent of Israel's annual GDP [gross domestic product], while the greater percentage of Palestinian farmers must rely on insufficient sources of rainwater for 90 percent of their agricultural activity. Desperate for water, Gazans also are overpumping this source, as their inadequate sewage networks continue to leak raw sewage into the supply. Medical sources in Gaza note an increase in kidney disease and other dangerous water-related illnesses. The U.N. estimates that in less than 15 years Gazans will not have access to drinkable water.

What little Palestinian water infrastructure there is falls regular victim to Israeli military assault. From the destruction of 140 wells in the 1967 war, to soldiers sniping at water tanks on family homes, to settlers vandalizing and polluting watercourses, to confiscation of wells for the building of "security" walls, Palestinians have no chance to improve their situation.

In July, Israel again launched a ground offensive into southern Lebanon. Is this another attempt to access the vital asset of the Litani River high on the agenda?

What is certain is that there will be no long-term security for any resident of the Middle East without fair distribution and a just solution to the sharing of water resources. Without regional cooperation on protecting rapidly depleting resources such as the Jordan River and the Dead Sea, not even Israel can count on secure water forever.

Periodical Bibliography

The following articles have been selected to supplement the diverse views presented in this chapter.

Tom Arrandale	"Disappearing Species: Cutting Deals," *CQ Researcher*, November 30, 2007.
Helen Beckett	"Want to Cut Costs? Then Go Green," *Computer Weekly*, May 1, 2007.
Dennis Behreandt	"Rethinking Green: There Are Legitimate Environmental Problems," *The New American*, August 6, 2007.
Lynn Braz	"The Next Big Green," *Whole Life Times*, December 2007.
The Economist	"Green Protectionism: Climate Change," November 17, 2007.
Elizabeth Kolbert	"Human Nature: The Talk of the Town," *The New Yorker*, May 28, 2007.
Christina Larson	"The Middle Kingdom's Dilemma: Can China Clean Up Its Environment Without Cleaning Up Its Politics?" *Washington Monthly*, December 2007.
Marianne Lavelle	"Water Woes," *U.S. News & World Report*, June 4, 2007.
James Martin and James E. Samels	"Painting the Ivory Towers Green: Creating Sustainable Campuses for the 21st Century," *University Business*, December 2007.
Jim Motavalli	"Sunshine Activism: Florida's Dramatic Turnabout on Climate Change," *Our Planet*, December 3, 2007.
Terry Sheridan	"Learning to Be Green," *Miami Daily Business Review*, September 5, 2007.
James Gustave Speth and Peter M. Haas	"A Second Attempt at Global Environmental Governance?" *The Environmental Forum*, September–October 2007.

OPPOSING
VIEWPOINTS®
SERIES

CHAPTER 4

What Methods Are Effective in Resolving International Conflicts?

Chapter Preface

When the Cold War ended in 1991 many politicians, diplomats, and scholars heralded the dawn of a new age of peace and stability in the world. With the United States and the Soviet Union no longer locked in a global struggle, many asserted that armed strife would increasingly become obsolete and conflicts would be resolved through mediation and arbitration. Former secretary of state and general Colin Powell claimed that the end of the superpower conflict would "usher in a new and brighter phase of history." However, through the 1990s, new conflicts and wars emerged. Many of these struggles were particularly brutal. They involved conflicts in which rival groups attempted to kill or displace people who were not of the same ethnicity or religion. For instance, in the Bosnian wars in the former Yugoslavia, more than 250,000 people were killed, and more than 1.3 million became refugees in fighting among ethnic Bosnians, Croats, and Serbs. In Rwanda, efforts by radical members of the Hutu tribe led to the deaths of more than 800,000 rival Tutsis and moderate Hutus. Former Republican congressman Tom DeLay, commenting on the Bosnian conflict, opined that "history teaches us that it is often easier to make war than peace."

The emergence of new struggles or the expansion of existing strife have led to new efforts to develop international bodies that could resolve conflict. When fighting erupted in Bosnia, many European leaders sought to have institutions such as the United Nations (UN) or the Organization for Security and Cooperation in Europe (OSCE) take the lead in crafting a negotiated settlement to end the violence. The UN authorized a peacekeeping mission and the OSCE deployed observers in an effort to stop the conflict. However, the efforts of these and other organizations failed to contain the war. Instead, it was only with the intervention of the North Atlantic Treaty Organization (NATO), a military alliance, that a settlement was reached in the ethnic conflict in 1995. NATO bombed Serb military positions surrounding the Bosnian capital of Sarajevo, which prompted the Serbs to agree to a peace accord. NATO peacekeepers were deployed and remained in Bosnia through 2007.

In the following viewpoint, scholars, officials, and a psychologist examine how countries and international organizations endeavor to use conflict resolution to end fighting. The essays explore the use of traditional diplomacy, psychology, and the role of national governments in efforts to resolve conflict.

I "I am a firm believer in peaceful conflict
resolution."

Conflict Resolution Provides a Way for Governments to Prevent Violence

Sonam Wangdu

In the following viewpoint, author Sonam Wangdu discusses the peaceful conflict resolution efforts used by the Tibetans while seeking independence from China. In lieu of a military uprising, the Tibetans have chosen peaceful demonstrations and assistance from other countries, including the United States, says Wangdu. The Tibetan approach is based in Buddhism, the nation's religion, which stresses nonviolence. Sonam Wangdu is the chair of the U.S. Tibet Committee, headquartered in New York City, and a former employee of the Tibetan Government-in-Exile.

As you read, consider the following questions:

1. Which famous Americans have inspired Wangdu in Tibet's efforts to seek independence from China?

2. How long does the author contend Tibet has existed as a nation?

Sonam Wangdu, "The China–Dalai Lama Dialogue: Prospects for Progress," Congressional-Executive Commission on China, Testimony, March 2006.

3. What two events made 2008 a good time to bring world attention to Tibet, according to Wangdu?

I was born in Kham, Tibet in 1942. My mother was forced to send me away to my uncles in central Tibet, in fear for my safety because it was rumored that young Tibetan boys were being shipped off to China for indoctrination. I was a child of 8 years old when I left my home. My eldest sister accompanied me across the country. My sister returned to Kham, and the next time we met again was after 36 years in Nepal. In 1954, my uncles brought me to India where I was enrolled in English-medium schools. I never returned home nor saw my Mother again.

Independence for Tibet

For 42 years, I have lived in the United States. I have raised my children here, and this country has been a host and a home to me, as well as an inspiration. I press on for independence for Tibet because I believe it can be achieved, and because that it is the only way to preserve real freedom for Tibetans.

I came to this country in 1964, and never left. I was deeply impacted by the Presidential elections taking place at that time. I watched with much excitement and even envy at the freedom that the citizens of this great country enjoyed in choosing their leaders and deciding their destinies. I read about the American Revolution, and was moved by the country's early leaders, in particular Patrick Henry, whose call "give me Liberty or give me Death" rang so true to my ears because my own countrymen were also laying down their lives for many of the same ideals upon which this country was founded. I was equally touched by President [John F.] Kennedy's pledge in his inaugural address that the U.S. "shall pay any price, bear any burden, meet any hardship, support any friend, oppose any foe, in order to assure the survival and

Buddhist and Conflict Resolution

Conflicts are not necessarily negative. As [founder of the Danish Centre for Conflict Resolution] Else Hammerich put it: "Conflicts are not negative, but life's challenges to us; they are part of the challenges of life. They can lead to social progress, more wisdom, frankness and understanding among people."

Obstacles to mental liberation like misunderstanding, hatred, delusion, and lust are inherent in the ignorant mind. The equivalent Tibetan Buddhist term for "ignorance" is dag-zin or egoistic mind. And the term conflict is equivalent to suffering in the sense that suffering causes emotional disruption. But while conflict is part of suffering, suffering itself is not conflict. For example, the sufferings of birth, old age, illness and death are not conflicts.

Tsering Dhondup,
"Buddhism and Conflict Resolution,"
Times of Tibet, *January 20, 2005.*

the success of liberty." It was not the hawkish stance that I admired in them but the firm commitment to liberty that is so essential for us Tibetans to reclaim our country.

The official policy of His Holiness the Dalai Lama and the Tibetan Government-in-Exile is to achieve a "genuine autonomy for all Tibetans living in the three traditional provinces of Tibet within the framework of the People's Republic of China." However, I believe the vast majority of Tibetans desire independence for our country because of reports from inside Tibet, and also because of the continuing arrests and imprisonment of Tibetans for even mentioning the name of the Dalai Lama.

Dalai Lama

An independent Tibet is fundamental to protecting the rights of the Tibetan people and bringing peace in the region. The Middle Way Approach is a concession to entreat dialogue with China. And to date, this policy has not led to meaningful dialogue. It has succeeded only in encouraging the PRC [People's Republic of China] to demand further concessions. Those who support the Middle Way Approach do so out of the highest regard for His Holiness the Dalai Lama. Those of us who dissent also do so out of the highest regard for His Holiness the Dalai Lama, a leader who has given us a lifetime of care and service characterized by extraordinary wisdom and compassion.

I would like to clarify that a dissenting opinion of this policy does not in any way indicate an opposition to either the Dalai Lama or the Tibetan Government-in-Exile. On the contrary, I believe that these are institutions we must have— the role of the Dalai Lama for us Tibetans has been vital to our cultural survival. It has been 57 years since China invaded Tibet; a long time in the span of a human life, but only a skipped beat in the history of a 2133 year old nation. In all these years the hope that Tibet will be free again has not diminished. Most of those senior government officials from all segments of our society, as well as many of my friends, family members and colleagues have now passed away, but the shared hope for freedom is still very much alive.

I was a child when Tibet became an occupied nation, but the generation that followed mine has grown up never having known an independent Tibet. They are truly the children of exile and occupation, yet they are tougher, better educated and more skeptical than us older Tibetans. They are the future of the movement. Figures like Tenzin Tsundue, who was recently profiled in the *New York Times Magazine*, Jamyang Norbu, author, and Lhasang Tsering, or the leaders of GuChuSum, an organization of former political prisoners now in exile, the Tibetan Youth Congress, or US-based organizations such as United States Tibet Committee, the Students for a Free Tibet and the International Tibet Independence Movement, to name a few, approach the Tibet-China situation with greater media literacy, technical savvy and an unwillingness to settle for anything less than total freedom for the country of their forebears. These are Tibetans, but they are also citizens of the world, with passports that reflect a United Nations–worthy diversity.

Peaceful Conflict Resolution

I am a firm believer in peaceful conflict resolution; and in the case of Tibet, it is imperative that both Tibet and China be earnest and sincere in searching for an acceptable resolution. But as the situation is now, the Middle Way Approach has not brought us any closer to a resolution of the Tibet issue:

- Contact with China in the new millennium has not shown any tangible progress apart from the Chinese leaders using these meetings to wage a public relations campaign to deflect criticism.

- Although the Chinese have entertained His Holiness the Dalai Lama's envoys, 4 times in China and once in Bern, Switzerland, they have refused to recognize their official purpose or who they represent.

- Even as the Chinese host these delegations, they continue to imprison Tibetans loyal to the Dalai Lama, and combined with the lack of improvement in human rights, they have shown they have no interest in loosening their grip on Tibet.

China is using these "talks" to lower the pressure from the US and the EU [European Union] who have been pushing for these talks for many years. It seems clear that the Chinese leaders are just going through the motions without showing any real interest in providing "genuine autonomy" for the people of Tibet. Yet the Tibetan Government-in-Exile, to create a "conducive environment" for the dialogues, continues to discourage her people and supporters from demonstrating against Chinese leaders during their visits overseas, and for the first time the officials of the New York–based Office of Tibet have been instructed not to participate in the March 10 demonstration this year [2006]. Concessions, be it voluntary or on demand, without reciprocity, are not inducements for serious talk. Despite these overtures and concessions by the Tibetan Government-in-Exile, China still maintains a hard line on Tibet, and the protests against China by exiled Tibetans continues. Tibetans are now even taking their fight into the heart of China where Wongpo Tethong, a Swiss Tibetan, on March 8 [2006], displayed a banner which read, "Hu, you can't stop us! 2008-Free Tibet.org" in Tiananmen Square. [Hu Jintao is the leader of China.] With all eyes on Beijing for the upcoming 2008 Olympic Games and the construction of the new railroad connecting China with Lhasa, the capital of Tibet, to promote tourism, this is the time and opportunity for the Tibetan Government-in-Exile and supporters to bring attention to Tibet's real situation.

If the US abides by [the] misperception of the progress of these talks, the danger exists that China will continue to forestall negotiations in the hopes for a post–Dalai Lama scenario where the issue will die with Him.

Rather than the issue dying away, there is a greater likelihood that the issue will destabilize, with future generations of very frustrated Tibetans resorting to other means to bring freedom to Tibet. The role and the position of the Dalai Lama has been a great stabilizer for the Tibetan community, the Free Tibet Movement, and even the world.

The Importance of Tibet

The world has grown smaller, and the issue of Tibet cannot be treated as an isolated case that affects the people of Tibet only.

This issue is now not simply a Tibetan issue, nor a nationalist issue, nor a human rights issue. The Tibet issue has now evolved into a global security and environmental issue.

It requires international attention to keep peace in the region. India's national security is at far greater risk now than ever before. We all saw this in the 1962 Chinese invasion of India from occupied Tibet. The dynamic hasn't changed; however, the destructive potential of a Sino-Indian [Chinese and Indian] conflict in modern times has the ability to go beyond the borders of these two most populous nations. Such a conflict would provide another dangerous rallying point for the world's clashing ideologies. It seems too clear that to allow Tibet to exist as an independent and neutral state is in humanity's best interest.

Tibet is located in a region of the world that is environmentally sensitive. Tibetans have for centuries learnt to live in harmony with nature. However, following the Chinese occupation of Tibet, widespread environmental destruction from massive and unplanned deforestation, farming and mining have had a profound effect on wildlife, soil erosion and global weather patterns. I am not an expert in this area but scientists have observed a direct link between natural vegetation on the Tibetan plateau and the stability of the monsoons, which is indispensable to the breadbasket of south Asia. They have also shown that the environment of the Tibetan plateau affects jet-steams which are related to the course of Pacific typhoons and the el Niño phenomenon. Based on these expert opinions, preserving Tibet's environment is just not in the interest of protecting an ancient and a unique culture, but it is also in the interest of the whole human race.

In our own lifetime we have seen the emergence of former colonies as independent states, and the inconceivable events of the fall of the Soviet Union and of the Berlin Wall [to end communism]. I believe Tibetans can have their national flag fly in the capitals of many nations and at the United Nations.

The goal is not easy to achieve but it is not impossible. We Tibetans must depend on our resolve, our commitment, our confidence to continue our just cause. My generation inherited a torn, ravaged and occupied Tibet, and for the sake of the future generations of Tibetans we have a duty to work hard to free Tibet.

> *"The international community remains unable to prevent the outbreak of war and the scope of action of many organizations is confined to limiting the negative effects of violence."*

Government and International Efforts at Conflict Resolution Usually Fail to Prevent Violence

Fred Tanner

In the following viewpoint, Fred Tanner contends that despite government and international initiatives, conflict resolution strategies often fail. Further, in spite of a growing body of literature and data on dispute resolution and attempts by world organizations, including the United Nations, to intervene in disputes, armed strife continues. In addition, Tanner argues that sometimes governments undermine international attempts to resolve conflicts in order to advance their own interests, even if it undermines peace efforts. Fred Tanner is an author and the deputy director of the Geneva Center for Security Policy.

Fred Tanner, "Conflict Prevention and Conflict Resolution: Limits of Multilateralism," *International Review of the Red Cross*, September 30, 2000. Copyright © 2000 International Committee of the Red Cross. Reproduced by permission.

As you read, consider the following questions:

1. According to the viewpoint, how many people were killed in conflicts in the 1990s?
2. What chapter of the United Nations Charter calls for parties involved in a conflict to try to settle it peacefully? What evidence does Tanner provide to prove the policy sometimes fails?
3. According to the viewpoint, what are some of the successful missions of the Organization for European Security and Cooperation?

Throughout the 1990s both practitioners and scholars have paid extensive attention to conflict prevention. Preventive actions are designed to resolve, manage, or contain disputes before they become violent. Conflict management, in turn, means the limitation, mitigation and containment of conflict. The notion of conflict prevention includes numerous activities such as conflict avoidance and conflict resolution, with techniques such as mediation, peace-keeping, peacemaking, confidence-building measures, and track-two diplomacy.

The concept of conflict prevention rests today on an impressive body of literature. Also, the United Nations (UN), regional organizations, State entities and non-governmental organizations [NGOs] have engaged in recent years in systematic "lessons learned" and "best practices" exercises with regard to failed missions or missed opportunities. Furthermore, numerous high profile and well financed research projects and blue ribbon reports have come up with policy recommendations that are directly feeding into the highest level of decision-making at the UN and other organizations.

Continuing Conflicts

But despite all these developments, conflict prevention remains an enigma. Conflicts continue to emerge and many of them turn violent. In the 1990s decade alone, approximately

5.5 million people were killed in almost 100 armed conflicts. These deadly conflicts have led to widespread devastation and regional instabilities, as well as large numbers of refugees. The international community remains unable to prevent the outbreak of war and the scope of action of many organizations is confined to limiting the negative effects of violence.

The main source of frustration for the international community is its inability to credibly and accurately predict and rapidly respond to conflicts that threaten to turn violent. This is due both to the complex dynamics of internal, ethnic and communal conflicts and to the reluctance of many States to take steps that involve risks and costs. Nevertheless, the increasing presence of international organizations and State and non-State entities in conflict-prone areas raises the hope that a multilateralization of conflict prevention could reduce the number of missed opportunities in the future. . . .

Taking Stock of Conflict Prevention Activities

International prevention of internal conflicts has been advocated since the end of the Cold War. In the light of several conflict management tasks successfully accomplished by the UN in the late 1980s and early 1990s (Namibia, Nicaragua, El Salvador), the UN Secretary-General's *Agenda for Peace* of 1992 devoted an entire chapter to conflict prevention. One of the novelties of his report was the creation of a conceptual link between various stages of conflict escalation and those policy actions that could remedy them. These include conflict prevention, dispute escalation prevention and the limitation of the spread of violence if it occurs. The last segment of these policy responses also opened the door to conflict management, an approach that established the conceptual ground for direct outside involvement to check escalating violence by using peaceful or even coercive means, if necessary.

The sobering experiences of the United Nations and the world at large in Somalia, Rwanda and Yugoslavia gave rise from the mid-1990s onward to the realization that there exists a clear need to reassess the role of the UN and other international entities in conflict prevention and conflict management. This realization was based on the recognition that conflict prevention needs a thorough understanding of conflicts and their relationship to failed States and State formation, and an institutional framework that can implement policy responses in a rapid and coherent manner. . . .

Toward Multilateralization of Conflict Prevention

The spread and global importance of internal conflicts in the 1990s, together with the increasing diversity of players in international affairs, has led to a certain multilateralization of conflict prevention efforts. This multilateralization presupposes that international and regional organizations, State and non-State entities would combine their efforts to fight the spread of deadly conflicts, in other words that all parties involved should accept a policy scheme that subscribes to a common vision on conflict resolution. But the diversity of mission mandates, the respective organizational turf, the bureaucratic red tape, national interests and conflicting views on conflict prevention and humanitarian actions set limits to effective multilateral action.

Among the various players, the United Nations remains the only institution with global legitimacy for conflict prevention. Yet regional organizations have been gaining importance in security cooperation over the last few years. While this type of cooperation is invaluable, the division of labour between the UN and regional organizations has run into trouble. For example, with regard to the NATO [North Atlantic Treaty Organization] military intervention in Kosovo, UN Secretary-General Kofi Annan warned that "conflict prevention, peacekeeping and peacemaking must not become an area of competition between the United Nations and regional organizations".

NGOs and humanitarian organizations play an integral and increasingly important role in conflict prevention, owing to their knowledge of and involvement in potential conflict areas. There is, however, an uneasy relationship between humanitarian organizations and other parties engaged in conflict prevention and peace implementation. In the final analysis, States remain the most important players in today's international system, and if their national interests are at stake, they may tend to short-cut international organizations in favour of international contact groups or unilateral action. . . .

The United Nations

Chapter VI of the UN Charter calls on those involved in a dispute to try to settle it peacefully, using a wide variety of diplomatic instruments. Article 99 of the Charter empowers the Secretary-General to bring to the attention of the Security Council "any matter which in his opinion may threaten the maintenance of international peace and security".

But the efficiency of these instruments is limited by the reluctance of the UN member States and particularly by the permanent members of the Security Council to confer more power upon the Secretary-General and his organization. The proposals for a UN Rapid Reaction Force, an important element for conflict prevention, has been thwarted for many years, even though eminent policy-makers and experts, such as Brian Urquhart, have called for it.

The defining question with regard to these forces, and to conflict prevention in general, is to what extent the United Nations can use its organization effectively for early warning and succeed in gaining sufficient commitments from member States for robust peace operations to be staged. Recent lessons learned from the developments in Rwanda and Srebrenica provide a very valuable insight into how the UN's approach to unfolding conflicts and deadly violence can be improved. Key issues concern the use of force, command and control, and the training and equipment of UN peace forces. The essential question remains the manner in which troop-contributing States are linked to the peace operation and how the Security Council is involved.

Rwanda

Both in Rwanda and in Bosnia, the UN failed to prevent genocide from taking place. In each case there was plenty of warning of the forthcoming mass killings, but the UN mishandled both of them. Two reports examining these cases were finally published in late 1999. Given the involvement of Kofi Annan as rapporteur of the Srebrenica mass killings and as one of the key persons to take partial blame at the UN for the handling of the unfortunate mission during the Rwanda genocide, these reports assume a high profile and could have a big impact on future policy-making in conflict prevention and conflict management.

In the case of Rwanda, the inadequate resources and the major countries' absence of political will were the underlying causes of failure. The report sums up that the UN presence in Rwanda was "not planned, dimensioned, deployed or instructed in a way which provided for a proactive and assertive role in dealing with a peace process in serious trouble". The mission lacked well-trained troops, functioning matériel and military capacity. The dearth of strong political commitments was made worse by the unilateral withdrawal of the national contingents during crucial moments of the unfolding crisis. In the case of Srebrenica, with the lack of commitments by outside powers to an effective resolution of the war in Bosnia, "a consensus absent in the Council, lacking a strategy, and burdened by an unclear mandate, UNPROFOR (UN Protection Force) was forced to chart its own course".

The Location of Armed Conflicts in 2006

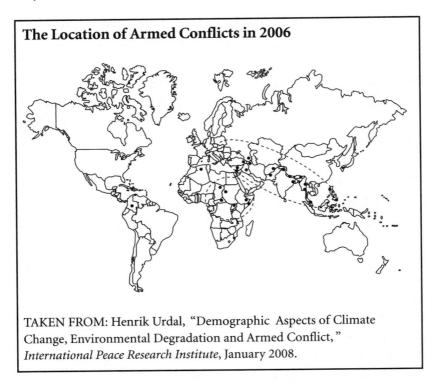

TAKEN FROM: Henrik Urdal, "Demographic Aspects of Climate Change, Environmental Degradation and Armed Conflict,"
International Peace Research Institute, January 2008.

There was early warning of the coming massacres: the Special UN Representative in Rwanda reported that one group was in clear violation of the peace agreement by stockpiling ammunition, distributing weapons and reinforcing positions in Kigali. Also, the now infamous cable by Force Commander General [Romeo] Dallaire refers unequivocally and urgently to information about planning and practical preparations for mass killings. The problem with early warning was twofold: first, the information was not processed correctly at the UN, owing to sloppiness and wrong lines of communication at its New York headquarters, and second, the "lack of capacity for intelligence analysis" contributed to an erroneous interpretation by the UN of the Arusha peace process and the intentions of the parties thereto. The lack of in-depth analysis of the political situation on the ground in Rwanda was clearly evidenced by the oversight of an alarming report by the Special Rapporteur of the Commission on Human Rights that—just two weeks before the UNAMIR (UN Assistance Mission in Rwanda) mission was launched—pointed to the deteriorating human rights situation and explicitly referred to the dangers of genocide.

Another lesson learned in conflict prevention is that the peace implementers should be able to continually adjust mission mandates, rules of engagement, troop strength and military capacities of peace missions to changing realities on the ground. The Rwanda mandate changed in nature from Chapter VI to Chapter VII of the Charter at a stage of the conflict when it would still have been possible to stop the genocide. But UNAMIR II failed, in the final analysis, because of the unwillingness of UN member States to provide troops for it. Two months after the Security Council agreed to the mission, UNAMIR II still only had 550 troops instead of 5,500. In the case of Srebrenica, after the Security Council had established the safe areas the force commander requested 34,000 troops, but finally had to settle for a "light option" with a minimal troop reinforcement of around 7,600 that was to be defended, if necessary, by NATO air strikes.

In its recommendations, the Rwanda Report points prominently to the need to improve the early warning capacity. It argues that it is essential to improve the ability of the UN Secretariat "to analyse and respond to information about possible conflicts, and its operational capability for preventive action". . . .

Regional Organizations

The *Agenda for Peace* makes a claim for more active use of regional organizations under the UN Charter's Chapter VIII, especially since the United Nations has become overstretched and overburdened. The contributions of ASEAN [Association of Southeast Asian Nations] in Cambodia, the Organization of American States and the Contadora Group in Central America, and the European Union, OSCE [Organization for Security and Co-operation in Europe], NATO and the Western European Union in the former Yugoslavia have indicated a potential that could make a substantial contribution to peace and stability. But this potential is not sufficiently exploited.

The only regional organization which has both normative and operational capabilities in conflict prevention is the Organization for Security and Co-operation in Europe. In 1990 the Charter of Paris for a New Europe mandated the OSCE to search for "ways of preventing, through political means, conflict which may emerge". As the incipient pan-European cooperative security structures were challenged and then invalidated by the Yugoslav wars, the OSCE realized that its role in conflict prevention lies more in the normative and soft security dimensions. In 1992, the OSCE created the Conflict Prevention Centre (CPC) to serve as a focal point in European early warning and dispute settlement. But, with minor exceptions, the CPC was bypassed during the explosion of deadly violence in the Balkans. States with vital stakes in the unfolding conflict apparently preferred to pursue their policies through the European Union, the UN and, ultimately, through international ad hoc contact groups.

A more successful initiative was the creation of a mandate for an OSCE High Commissioner on National Minorities, tasked to provide early warning and early prevention in minority conflicts. The role of the High Commissioner has been more successful than the CPC because of his ability to address structural causes of conflict directly with the parties concerned. His sustained engagement with the Baltic States, for instance, helped to defuse tension over the status of Russian minorities.

Lastly, the OSCE agreed to engage in long-term missions in potential trouble spots where latent tensions could erupt into violence and war. It currently has missions posted in 17 countries in the Balkans, the Caucasus, Central and Eastern

Europe and Central Asia. These missions have been successful in countries such as Estonia, Latvia, Macedonia, Moldova and the Ukraine. Conversely, their presence failed to have the desired effect in other areas such as Bosnia, Chechnya, Georgia, Tajikistan and Kosovo where, despite their work, violence has prevailed. The experience of the OSCE in conflict prevention shows that long-term missions and discreet work on structural questions such as democracy-building, human and minority rights and the promotion of civil society are more suitable for regional organizations than attempts to find quick-fixes for the direct causes of conflict.

The Reality of Conflict Prevention

The reality of conflict prevention is that it is neither risk-free nor cheap. Preventive diplomacy is viable only if there are parties willing to pledge assistance and provide guarantees. Local parties in dispute almost always need outside backing to credibly guarantee the implementation of agreements. The States that are prepared to assume such responsibilities are primarily stakeholders in the hot spot areas. Their interests may be geopolitical or affected by the politically costly effects of violence, such as refugee flows, regional destabilization and pressure by exile groups. The cost factors, both politically and financially, will induce such States to give credible commitments. Referring to the unfolding Kosovo crisis in 1998, the *Economist* wisecracked that successful prevention "does not win votes, but failed intervention loses buckets of them".

> "Many social scientists, psychologists, psychiatrists, social workers, and those trained in conflict resolution, have much to contribute to a deeper understanding of current terrorist mentality."

Psychologists Can Play an Important Role in International Conflict Resolution

Mark J. Hovee

This viewpoint explores the importance of psychological factors in international conflict resolution efforts in areas such as Iraq or in the ongoing Arab-Israeli conflict. Specifically, the viewpoint examines the benefits of incorporating mental health professionals into alternative dispute resolution initiatives. It also stresses the necessity of including alternative cultural perspectives into conflict resolution endeavors, especially as a means to better understand the motivations for terrorism. Mark J. Hovee is a clinical psychologist in Paintsville, Kentucky, and an officer in the U.S. Army Reserve.

Mark J. Hovee, "Diplomatic Efforts in the Middle East: Can Psychologists and Conflict Resolution Specialists Contribute to the Negotiation Process?," *The Online Journal of Peace and Conflict Resolution*, vol. 7, January 2006. www.trinstitute.org/ojpcr/ 7_1hovee.pdf. Reproduced by permission of the author.

As you read, consider the following questions:

1. According to the viewpoint, what is the major "obstacle" that impedes mental health professionals from having a larger role in conflict management?

2. What does Hovee assert is unique about the 2003 conference in Dubai, United Arab Emirates?

3. What does the author claim was his main duty while stationed in Germany?

The U.S. deployment of troops to Afghanistan initially, and subsequently to Iraq, has profoundly engaged my thoughts and sentiments like few other prolonged situations have ever done. The impact has been particularly dramatic since I am also a clinical psychologist in the Army Reserve. But, as much as my adrenal glands were ignited in anticipation of being activated "down range," it turned out my number remained dormant, leastwise throughout the first year of the war.

Psychology and Conflict Resolution

What has persistently gnawed on my senses throughout the whole ordeal has been the question of whether the research and clinical sides of psychological practice, as well as those trained in conflict resolution, can have any substantial contribution to make to the current situation that exists in the Middle East today. Despite the possibility psychological analysis and clinical "know how" will be relegated to "arm chair theorizing," I find myself considering the notion again that psychology may have much to offer to the current conflict in Iraq, Israel, and the Middle East as a whole, particularly when various "avenues of approach" are made available.

On a much smaller scale, I am reminded of a psychiatric hospital I have been affiliated with. There have been several departmental turf battles, interpersonal conflicts, long-standing resentments, managerial disregard for adequate staffing, and what can be considered a widespread state of staff apathy and burnout. These problems have been noted for years, despite the presence of psychologists with considerable skills in conflict resolution, effective team building, and management-employee problem solving strategies.

One key obstacle preventing behavioral health professionals from having a positive impact is that they have rarely been given a "green light" from management to address these issues. So, whether the setting is a psychiatric hospital, for instance, or in an international context, the knowledge and skills psychologists possess regarding human behavior are likely to have greater difficulties being realized when a viable role has not been designated for them.

Global Conflicts

My difficulty since 9/11 [the September 11, 2001, terrorist attacks on America] has been to find opportunities where psychologists and conflict resolution professionals can effectively exercise the "tools of their trade" in such a way that their expertise and proposed interventions actually impact the decisions of policy makers in the United States, other countries in the Middle East, and many other countries associated with the events in the Middle East.

During the initial stages of Operation Iraqi Freedom, I attended a local Rotary Club meeting where a retired three star General gave a presentation on military steps being employed in the Iraqi theatre of operations. He responded cordially to a question posed regarding how much thought military leaders had given to addressing the prospect of another generation of terrorists emerging in years to come. His response was to note the armed forces were still operating in a reactive mode. It was therefore his assessment the military by and large had not yet been able to seriously evaluate the psychological forces at work which might lead to another wave of fresh terrorists "down the road" (i.e., terrorists "in the wings," so to speak).

As understandable as it is that the primary focus of the military has been directed toward a decisive defeat of terrorist objectives, the simultaneous focus on the "larger landscape" is one particularly well suited to psychologists. Many social scientists, psychologists, psychiatrists, social workers, and those trained in conflict resolution, have much to contribute to a deeper understanding of current terrorist mentality, the necessary ingredients needed to perpetuate more terrorism in the years to come, and conversely approaches likely to diminish future terrorist recruits.

2003 Conference

In December 2003, an opportunity for psychologists emerged with regard to events in the Middle East. The very first Middle East/North Africa Regional Conference in Psychology convened for close to a week in Dubai, United Arab Emirates (UAE). This conference was largely attended by psychologists and other mental health providers from various countries in the Gulf region and the Middle East as a whole, as well as a few from assorted distant countries. I was one of a small handful of American participants at the conference. Even though Israelis would not normally be allowed into an Arab country like the UAE, arrangements were made for several psychologists/academicians from Israel to bypass the normal entry point through Customs and be present for the conference.

A stated purpose of the conference was to address what impact psychology could have on the various conflicts in the region. However, given the scientific nature of the conference, the focus was predominantly directed to research-based presentations. Some exceptions did occur, such as a presentation by a Palestinian therapist describing her work with Palestinian women traumatized by the death of their spouses in Israel. However, very little attention was given to the current problem of American soldiers engaged in armed conflict within two Arab countries, and how psychologists might help to ameliorate the extent of the conflict and the rising death toll for indigenous Afghanis, Iraqis, American soldiers, other Coalition forces, and contract workers alike.

I also received approval to conduct an impromptu networking session to facilitate ongoing connections following the conclusion of the conference. This at least allowed a forum for me to inform the group of nine participants my interest in the roles psychologists might have regarding peacemaking in the region. My proposed area of interest did not spawn the kind of dialogue I had hoped for. Many factors very likely accounted for this lack of enthusiastic feedback—two reasons possibly being my "outsider" status and their view of the intractable nature of these regional conflicts.

My exposure to a more Arab approach to the field of psychology through my involvement at this conference did prove to be useful, even regarding the question I was attempting to find an answer to. For one thing, a dominant theme of the conference impressed itself on me—this being a profound distrust Arab practitioners appeared to have toward a westernized form of psychology being imposed on them. As has increasingly come to the fore with many cultural and ethnic groups, a number of participants were noting that the Arab world deeply steeped in Islamic values had need of developing their own culture-specific psychology.

Alternative Views of Conflict Resolution

This suggested to me that any viable peacemaking and conflict resolution strategies would likely be enhanced by incorporating an Arab/Islamic worldview. Otherwise, any conflict resolution approaches employed by psychologists would easily be considered irrelevant, or at least flawed, in fostering reduced tensions in the region.

All the American-bred optimism in the universality of their democratic principles and psychological understanding

Violence in Colombia as a Way of Life

Violence is permanent in the confrontation between the guerrilla, the government, the mob and paramilitaries. This undeclared civil war has taken the life of 70,000 people and displaced 600,000 in *40 years* of war. But these are just the *direct* victims of the conflict. Indirectly, the conflict has exacerbated the widespread violence of everyday life in Colombia: 30,000 people or so are murdered *each year* in the streets of the principal cities of the country. In 1997, Cali—the second biggest city of the country—recorded 90 murders per 100,000 people. Bogota, the capital, recorded 49 murders per 100,000. These figures outran even Caracas's 48, Rio de Janeiro's 34, Mexico City's 12 and Chicago's 30. . . .

The ability of the Colombian State to provide for the well being and the security of its citizens has been deteriorating dramatically during the last twenty years. Today, violence in general is a far-reaching illness in Colombia.

Camilo A. Azcarate,
"Psychosocial Dynamics of the Armed Conflict in Colombia,"
Online Journal of Peace and Conflict Resolution, *March 1999.*

of human beings could in the final analysis serve as an obstacle for the peace process in the Middle East. Embarrassing as it is to admit, I too have to acknowledge the inclination of exporting my own understanding of psychological principles onto the Arab world, and of course expecting a positive outcome.

It just so happened my presence at the conference coincided with the capture of [Iraqi leader] Saddam Hussein. The timing was fortuitous beyond the obvious in the sense it enabled me to discover another form of thinking in the Arab world quite different from what I was familiar with in the West. It appeared one reaction amongst some Arabs involved a feeling of ambivalence. While relieved a dictatorial leader was being brought to justice, there seemed to be a concern that even an Arab tyrant should not be publicly humiliated— this being especially the case at the hands of a Western power.

One woman I talked with about it indicated her displeasure that Saddam's extended family, particularly the children, would be subjected to endless replays of Saddam's disheveled and haggard looking countenance—a shaming experience for any Arab family to experience. The importance of preserving family honor struck me as a critical piece of effective work in this area of the world, and one which so unwittingly from a western mind-set could be violated.

As much as the conference expanded my horizons as a psychologist with international interests, and an American one at that, the lingering question remains in force. It is a much tougher arena for psychologists to function in, this being the diplomatic front, than the more familiar terrain of clinical work and research/teaching. It may be the formal invitations some of us keep awaiting may be long in materializing, just as has been the case with the psychiatric hospital referred to earlier.

Psychologists as Peacemakers

That some pioneering psychologists and conflict resolution professionals have found workable avenues from which to operate as effective peacemakers says a lot about their tenacity to "stay the course," even when the progress made may occur on the fringes of thorny "flashpoints" that career diplomats/ politicians, government officials and military leaders find so problematic in forging out agreements, deals, cease fires, and diminishment of conflicts.

Still, it is worth noting the research work for this article did not yield any evidence that psychologists and conflict resolution specialists had ever participated directly in the Arab-Israeli negotiations. This absence of involvement was additionally maintained by two presenters of Palestinian-Israeli issues at the International Conference of Political Psychology in July 2004.

This article could not go to "press" quickly enough before my involvement with Middle Eastern affairs would take another unexpected and divergent turn. The Army did in fact decide to call me up for military duty. Rather than to the "sandbox," as military personnel often refer to the Middle East, my assignment has been to Landstuhl, Germany. The need for psychologists assigned to the outpatient psychiatric wing of the regional hospital has increased. This is due in part to the growing volume of soldiers coming in from Afghanistan and Iraq—Landstuhl being used as a kind of weigh station before soldiers move on to the U.S. or back to their original unit "down range."

My clinical skills were tested in new ways, such as evaluations conducted by me pertaining to the mental health stability of soldiers pulled from varied operational areas in the Middle East. Determinations had to be made whether such soldiers could return to their units in the Middle East and once again be considered viable team members.

There were also the family members left behind in Germany who struggled in various ways with being separated and uncertain about the future. My schedule two days a week, and subsequently expanded to three days a week, placed me at the Family Health Clinic, Baumholder Army Post where large components of the 1st Armored Division had been deployed to Iraq for a year originally, and then an additional extension for up to 120 days. My caseload there had been primarily comprised of spouses dealing with the stresses of being apart from their "soldier spouse," their own mental-emotional struggles, and managing their children alone over this extended time frame. However with the return of most of the

Brigade from Iraq in July 2004, I worked more with soldiers adjusting to the very different demands of military life in the "rear."

Iraq

The reality of the escalation of tension in Iraq impacted me on two fronts. One front was the steady barrage of media highlighting the mounting drama with religious/political groups such as the Shiites and Sunnis, along with other "flash-points" like Baghdad, Fallujah, and the January 2005 elections. The other front involved the soldiers themselves landing on the "Landstuhl doorstep," often with little more than the rumpled uniform they wore during the initial days back and a rather bewildered and lost look in their eyes.

Again the haunting question came back to me in the midst of my daily clinical work with soldiers and family members. It pressed upon me even more pointedly as U.S. soldiers contended with an escalation of insurgent violence against many different individuals and groups considered to be cooperating with the U.S. This personal inquiry seemed to burn in my mind as again the world watched, military and civilian alike, with anticipation and dread that the level of violence and instability in future months could escalate to more tragic proportions. And yes, the Army hospital here in Landstuhl had learned to anticipate heightened trauma—medical and mental health staff alike—soberly prepared for those episodes of an increased volume of physically and mentally compromised soldiers flooding in from "down range."

Is it possible properly trained psychologists and conflict resolution professionals really could positively impact the outcome of conflicts as primed for protracted bloodletting as with Iraq and the Israeli-Palestinian struggle? The best that can be done thus far, it would seem, is to pose the hypothesis with the hope that greater levels of applied research might occur. It can further be hypothesized the area of negotiations most compatible with the training and skills of clinical psychologists and conflict resolution specialists pertains to the "process work" of the talks as opposed to the content domain.

The Need for Interaction

Of course, in order to secure the most meaningful research on this question, psychologists and conflict resolution professionals would need to be brought into the arena as genuine contributors where actual negotiations and decisions are made— ones determining the course the differing sides will take in a conflict. Arriving at this point does not have to be in the distant future, as there remains time for such experimentation even germane to the current conflict in Iraq between the American military, the terrorist groupings, disillusioned Iraqis, factional religious groups, and outside Arab entities.

I have gone through graduate school and practiced as a psychologist during a time when the horizons for psychologically related endeavors has dramatically expanded. This implies a growing recognition that practitioners of psychological principles can positively benefit human enterprises across the spectrum, even with regard to international conflicts and wars.

The American Psychological Association (APA), has highlighted this potential with what is termed "peace psychologists," recognizing a need for standardizing this area of practice to insure adequate training and expertise. It may be the time is nearing when one of the oldest dilemmas known to humankind—this being intractable conflicts culminating in much bloodshed—will become assessable to the strange, but penetrating tools of psychologists and conflict resolution specialists who regularly practice the art of negotiation, compromise, and identifying with the merits of both sides within the confines of private offices, conference rooms and the like.

"*Most explanations attribute mediator effectiveness . . . to the mediator's ability to . . . help disputants overcome their psychological biases and misperceptions.*"

International Conflict Resolution Initiatives Work Best When They Utilize Third Parties

Robert W. Rauchhaus

This viewpoint by Robert W. Rauchhaus examines why mediation and conflict resolution are effective when undertaken by third parties, such as international organizations or other countries. Central to the success of outside parties, says Rauchhaus, is accurate information and an ability to provide unbiased assistance to both sides in a dispute. The viewpoint identifies four indicators of success in international disputes and the likelihood of achieving the optimum outcomes. Robert W. Rauchhaus is an assistant professor of political science at the University of California, Santa Barbara, and the editor of the 2001 book Explaining NATO Enlargement.

Robert W. Rauchhaus, "Asymmetric Information, Mediation, and Conflict Management," *World Politics*, vol. 58, January 2006, pp. 207–41. Copyright © 2006 The Johns Hopkins University Press. Reproduced by permission.

As you read, consider the following questions:

1. According to the viewpoint, what is one of the "root causes of war"?

2. As stated in the viewpoint, are third parties more likely to use a single conflict management approach or multiple techniques?

3. What are the four indicators of success in a conflict, as listed in the viewpoint?

Civil wars and interstate disputes are frequently subject to mediation efforts by third parties. Scholars and analysts have engaged in extensive evaluation of the contextual and process variables associated with successful mediation, but much less is known about the underlying causal mechanisms of mediation. Most explanations attribute mediator effectiveness to the use of carrots and sticks or to the mediator's ability to link issues or help disputants overcome their psychological biases and misperceptions. . . .

Asymmetric Information

In the international relations field, game theorists have identified asymmetric information as one of the root causes of war. The dilemma created by private information and strategic incentives to bluff creates a prime opportunity for third parties to step in and act as mediators. If third parties possess private information about one or more of the disputants' capabilities or resolve, then sharing the information should reduce the likelihood of war.

Although the role of asymmetric information is central to formal rationalist explanations of war, it receives virtually no treatment in the traditional literature on mediation. Studies generally focus on establishing a relationship between effective mediation and structural or contextual variables, such as conflict intensity or the nature of issues in dispute, rather than on the causal mechanisms of mediation. Recent studies have generated more robust statistical findings, but they too have done so without tracing causal pathways and developing a theory of mediation effectiveness. Another important line of research has explained why and under what conditions third parties chose to mediate, but not why or when mediation will prove effectively. . . .

Civil wars and interstate disputes are frequently subject to numerous conflict-management efforts. A single third party may employ a number of conflict-management techniques, or a number of different third parties may intervene simultaneously or sequentially using a variety of conflict-management techniques. If a data set includes information on only one form of conflict management, then a statistical estimator may be biased because it will register the effects of omitted conflict-management activities. Thus, evaluating the effects of mediation is very difficult. . . .

Indicators of Success

Defining "success" is an inherently normative undertaking. For example, is the UN [United Nations] peacekeeping operation in Cyprus a success or failure? One might argue that it is a success in terms of preventing fighting but a failure in terms of addressing the underlying issue and ending the dispute. Similarly, mediators may generate dozens of cease-fires, as they have often done in the Middle East, but few of these cease-fires lead to a temporary cessation of hostilities, let alone to permanent ones.

To provide analysts and policymakers with useful information and allow the results of this study to be compared with previous studies, tests are performed using four different indicators of success. *Escalation* indicates whether disputes escalate to a higher level of crisis or fighting. *Peaceful Settlement*, by contrast, indicates whether a specific phase of a dispute ends with a partial or comprehensive settlement. Two additional indicators are added for both substantive and methodological

Human Rights Education Is Essential

Many government international agencies, and NGOs [non-governmental organizations] today are faced with the daunting task of re-establishing peace and order in post-war societies. In so doing, they have, at least in the abstract, appeared to recognize not only that human rights are an essential component of just societies, but that human rights education is a necessary element in the process of reestablishing stable and just post-war societies. Hence, human rights have become an important concept in both popular and diplomatic language. Human Rights Education (HRE) is based on the premise that human rights will reduce violence within society, if understood as generally accepted principles and rules of society expressed and adapted to a particular society and culture.

> *Tania Bernath, Tracey Holland, and Paul Martin,*
> *"How Can Human Rights Education*
> *Contribute to International Peace-Building?"*
> Conflict Resolution Journal, *Fall 2002.*
> *www.sipa.columbia.edu/cicr/research/journal/archive/index.html.*

reasons. *Hostilities* is added because it specifically measures whether a dispute escalates to armed combat. *Dispute End* is added because it more directly measures whether a dispute is terminated in its present phase. . . .

Light mediation, which targets asymmetric information, emerges as an effective form of conflict management. Indeed, it is the most effective of the seven conflict-management techniques evaluated [in this study]. It is the only conflict-management technique that registers substantively and statistically significant effects for all four of our indicators of success (escalation, peaceful settlements, hostilities, and disputes ending). Of all the conflict-management techniques tested, light mediation is also the only one that reduces the chance of hostilities and increases the chances that a dispute will terminate in its present phase.

"Rice's class taught us that C students rush to war, while A students work diligently and patiently toward peaceful solutions to international problems."

Diplomacy Is Effective in Resolving International Conflicts

Juliet Johnson

In the following viewpoint, Juliet Johnson argues that armed aggression is seldom the best way to resolve conflicts. Instead, she recommends diplomacy to settle differences. Johnson uses the example of the United States' approach to the Iraq War to illustrate her main contentions and underscore the benefit of diplomatic action over military action in conflict resolution. Johnson is an assistant professor of political science at Loyola University in Chicago.

As you read, consider the following questions:

1. In the viewpoint, what language has President Bush used in describing the war on terror and how is it likely to impact the resolution of conflicts in the Iraq War?

Juliet Johnson, "A Lesson in Diplomacy," *The Nation*, March 18, 2003. Reproduced by permission.

2. Why does the author say it is important to seek international support in managing international conflicts?

3. According to the author, what actions taken by the United States have harmed the nation's credibility?

Back in the late 1980s, Condoleezza Rice—then just a lowly associate professor—taught one of the best courses I took as a Stanford undergraduate. Although she called it "The Role of the Military in Politics," the most memorable class sessions involved a lengthy crisis simulation exercise designed to teach the fine art of avoiding war. She split the large class into several independent groups, with each group subdivided into key Washington foreign policy roles. My group had a President, a Vice President, a National Security Adviser, a Defense Secretary, a CIA Director, Joint Chiefs and several members of Congress. I was the Secretary of State. Our mission: to resolve an emerging international crisis peacefully if possible, by force if necessary. Sound familiar?

Professor Rice's simulation presciently challenged us to contain an impending civil war in Yugoslavia that, if inflamed, threatened to spill over into neighboring countries. All of the groups tried to achieve the same outcome—a peaceful resolution of the conflict—but few succeeded. Rather, a group's result depended on the strategies it used to pursue the goal. As we navigated the treacherous waters of (simulated) international diplomacy, our group learned three valuable lessons that Professor Rice's current colleagues in the Bush Administration seem to be neglecting.

Three Important Lessons

Rhetoric matters: During the simulation, I sent an unintentionally condescending message to the Greek government. Only by apologizing immediately and profusely did I manage to salvage our diplomatic mission. If even accidental slights have unfortunate consequences, how much harm can come from intentionally inflammatory rhetoric? When George W. Bush used the word "crusade" to describe US antiterrorism efforts, it unwittingly evoked images of Christian warriors marching to rescue the Holy Land from Islamic infidels. Yet rather than retreating from this rhetorical stance, Bush has fanned the flames by describing the current conflict with Iraq in biblical terms, repeatedly invoking the Christian God and calling Iraq an agent of evil. If Bush actually wants to fuel a "clash of civilizations," this is a good way to start. As then-candidate Bush himself said in the second presidential debate, "if we're an arrogant nation, [other countries] will view us that way, but if we're a humble nation, they'll respect us." Which brings us to lesson number two. . .

Seek international support: In our simulation, the most successful groups immediately reached out to allies and to international organizations in order to build a consensus on how to resolve the crisis. Similarly, candidate Bush acknowledged the need for multilateral cooperation on Iraq during that same second presidential debate, stating that "[Saddam Hussein] is a danger, and. . .it's going to be important to rebuild that coalition to keep the pressure on him." Yet as President, Bush has taken an "it's my way or the highway" approach. The Administration made it clear from the beginning that US policy on Iraq would not be influenced by its European allies or the United Nations, and has accused doubting foreign leaders of cowardice. Bush's March 17 ultimatum conclusively signaled the failure of diplomacy. This is coercion, not consultation. But perhaps even more important in coalition-building is lesson number three. . .

Maintain credibility: Not surprisingly, the groups in our class simulation that made the clearest and most credible arguments in defense of their policies typically gained the most support for them. As Bush noted in, yes, that second presidential debate, "I think credibility is going to be very important in the future in the Middle East." Yet the Administration has

The Camp David Accords—Diplomacy in Action

President [Jimmy] Carter's efforts to mediate peace in the Middle East are also a textbook example of international mediation. . . .

The Camp David Talks opened on September 5, 1978. At the outset, there was a tremendous gap between the positions of the two states: [Israeli prime minister Menachem] Begin repeated the old hard-line position, while [Egyptian president Anwar] Sadat stuck to his positions on the question of land and sovereignty; Egypt would reclaim every inch of disputed land, and fully exert its sovereignty over these regions. In the course of debate between the two states, Carter did not clearly state his position, using several different approaches to pushing the dialogue along. Both of these factors helped to establish trust between the parties. In the course of discussions between them, Carter found new ways of changing the context of relations between the countries by paying careful attention to their respective unique characteristics.

Qi Heixia, "A Comparison of the Effectiveness of International Conflict Mediation Strategies," The Chinese Journal of International Politics 2007, vol. 1, pp. 589–622.

not convincingly explained to the international community why it thinks Saddam Hussein represents a uniquely immediate threat.

Lessons Ignored During the Iraq War

In particular, two avowed US motives for insisting upon regime change undermine the Administration's credibility: Iraq's alleged Al Qaeda connection and its human rights violations.

The evidence tying Saddam Hussein to Al Qaeda is embarrassingly flimsy. Osama bin Laden has publicly expressed contempt for the secular Hussein, and several other countries—most notably Saudi Arabia, a close US ally—have much tighter Al Qaeda connections. As a result, many suspect that Bush is merely using the September 11 tragedy to justify his long-held desire to oust Hussein.

The Bush Administration's alleged concern for human rights violations in Iraq is equally unconvincing. The Taliban in Afghanistan had a reprehensible human rights record for years, but this did not become an important issue for the Administration until after September 11. Liberia, Burma, Turkmenistan and many other authoritarian states repress their people in appalling ways, but US troops are not massed at their borders. Such weak arguments for singling out Iraq breed cynicism and confusion in the international community and encourage speculation that less honorable motives are driving US foreign policy. The Administration is on the brink of war without having made a good case for removing Saddam Hussein from power.

(Our group also learned a fourth lesson—Congress can be safely ignored. The students playing members of Congress in the simulation had a frustrating week, as the rest of us made all of the important decisions. However, the Bush Administration understands this lesson.)

In short, Rice's class taught us that C students rush to war, while A students work diligently and patiently toward peaceful solutions to international problems. When the Iraqi crisis has ended, what grade will the current Administration have earned?

| "Opening talks with [our potential enemies], as many have suggested, cannot in itself be enough."

War Is Sometimes Necessary to Resolve International Conflicts

Clark S. Judge

In this viewpoint, Clark S. Judge argues that military force is often needed to resolve international disputes. The author lists a series of conflicts in the twentieth century in which military force was used to topple repressive regimes. He also argues that the United States must continue to fight and ultimately win the conflict in Iraq because that struggle is actually part of a longer fight between the forces of repression and those of liberal democracy led by the United States. Clark S. Judge is a former speechwriter for President Ronald Reagan and is currently the managing editor of the White House Writer's Group.

As you read, consider the following questions:

1. According to the viewpoint, what six empires dominated global politics in the nineteenth century?

2. Who founded the terrorist group, the Society of Muslim Brotherhood, according to Judge?

3. What country does the author identify as the most serious future threat to the United States?

The president [George W. Bush] and his senior advisers attempted last summer [2006] to define our adversary when they referred to [terrorist organization] al Qaeda and like groups as "Islamofascists." It was a short-lived attempt, but the president might have been onto something. While there may not be a strict ideological correspondence between Islamism [a radical version of Islam] and fascism, there is a strong historical relationship between the two—and between Islamism and Communism, too. All three ideologies arose from a common historical upheaval; all three share common pathologies; and all three dissent from the democratic consensus that individual happiness is the measure of social good, that popular sovereignty is the foundation of political legitimacy, and that the protection of life, liberty, and property is the end of just government.

The global strife of the last hundred years consists of four episodes: World War I, World War II, the Cold War, and the current conflict. Each involved distinct adversaries with distinct ideologies for distinct periods of time. Viewed through a broader lens, however, these wars can be seen as part of a single global upheaval, a new "hundred years war." This perspective tells us much about the war in Iraq and the broader war on terror.

The Collapse of a World Order

Global politics in the late 19th century was a story of six empires: German, Austrian, Russian, Ottoman, French, and British. While this world spawned the Crimean War and the Franco-Prussian War, it was mostly peaceful and its players stable. None tried to deliver a deathblow to another. That all ended with World War I. A foolish Kaiser [Wilhelm II] and the Prussian military elite sought to achieve lasting dominance in the decades-old contest—up to that point primarily diplomatic—which historian A. J. P. Taylor termed "the struggle for the mastery of Europe."

The outcome of the war was nothing like what the Kaiser intended. Americans see it as the moment the United States stepped onto the global stage, as indeed it was. Equally consequential, though, was the collapse of four of the six major 19th-century powers. By the mid-1920s, the German and Austro-Hungarian Empires, the Russian Empire, and the Ottoman Empire were no more. In each, the old monarchy had been abolished. Germany had lost the provinces (seized from France after the Franco-Prussian War) of Alsace and Lorraine, the industrial Ruhr Valley, and its overseas possessions, while Austro-Hungary had lost everything outside of Austria. The Russian Empire had collapsed into revolution and civil war. The Ottoman Empire was permanently removed from the global scene, and in its place were seven countries and a League of Nations mandate.

Filling the Void

The history of global, and particularly European, affairs since then has been largely the record of democratic countries coping with the pathological successors to these collapsed regimes, and with the countries of the Great Game area between the Russian and Ottoman territories. Autocratic and totalitarian governments emerged from the upheavals that followed imperial implosion: Nazism in Germany and Austria; Communism in Russia; and, in the Middle East, after a period of monarchies, Nasser's and now Murbarak's Egypt, bin-Saud's Saudi Arabia, Baathist Syria and Iraq, and Khomeini's Iran. In the old Ottoman domain, only the core country, Turkey, and the post–World War II state of Israel established anything approaching popular sovereignty, with its attendant claim of governmental legitimacy.

In each of these emergent regimes, terror quickly became a prime instrument of power, as did anti-Semitism. All the imperial remnants used hatred of minorities, particularly Jews, to prop themselves up with the majority groups on which they had such an uncertain hold.

Oppression

In each region, cults of death became a grim norm. The Soviets and the Nazis had their concentration camps, purges, and holocausts—killing orgies that were mirrored in different forms in the Middle East from the 1970s to today. There also emerged a celebration of death similar to the "you love life, we love death" rantings of current terrorists. A particularly famous moment came in 1936, at a meeting at the University of Salamanca in Spain. In response to a speech by an adversary, Nazi ally and Francoist General Milan-Astray shouted "Viva la Muerte!" The poet Miguel de Unamuno, the university's rector, was presiding. He replied: "This is the temple of intelligence and I am its high priest. You are profaning its sacred domain. You will succeed, because you have enough brute force. But you will not convince. To convince it is necessary to persuade, and to persuade you will need something you lack: reason and right in the struggle."

Expansionism with global ambitions became the challenge which each region eventually posed to the United States and its allies. The Germanic successor regimes brought us World War II; the Russians, the Cold War; and now, the successors to the Ottomans and the rulers of the Great Game region [Central Asia] have given us the war on terror. Iran's pretensions are overt, as were [Iraqi leader] Saddam Hussein's—ambitions that gave them a unifying cry with which to unite their peoples. In most countries of the region, promises to destroy Israel likewise offer ballast to unstable governments. Al Qaeda and other terrorist groups, though not states themselves, serve as surrogates for states afraid to take on the United States directly. Such groups are also state pretenders, like the Nazis or Soviets before their seizures of power, making the prospect of expansion, and with it expiation of past humiliations, part of their appeal.

A Shared Heritage

The links of the Nazis, Fascists, and Soviets with the Islamists, and others in the Middle East go beyond shared pathologies.

For example, as detailed on the website *Palestine Facts, Haj Amin al-Husseini*, the infamous Mufti of Jerusalem during much of the British mandate, allied himself with Nazi Germany in the 1930s and received financing from the SS [Schutzstaffel, the Nazi police unit] from 1936 through 1939. In 1937, after the exposure of his role in terrorism within Palestine, he fled to Syria and from there to Iraq. In 1941, he helped organize a pro-Nazi revolt in Baghdad [Iraq's capital], following which he fled to Berlin. There he became an advocate of and cheerleader for the Holocaust. After the war, he sought exile in Egypt, where he was received and celebrated as a hero of Arab nationalism. Fear of backlash from the Arab world kept the Allies from prosecuting him for war crimes. Upon his death, his leadership in the radical nationalist Palestinian Arab community passed to his nephew and protégé, Yasser Arafat.

[Nazi leader Adolf] Hitler also had an influence elsewhere in the formerly Ottoman world. In his recently published volume, *The Foreigner's Gift*, Lebanese-born scholar Fouad Ajami writes of the 1930s and 1940s: "[T]here was a Berlin-Baghdad corridor. It brought to Iraq the ways and culture and hysteria of the Third Reich and inspired, if that is the word, a generation or two of political men to ideologies of absolutism and violence." As a young man, Michel Aflaq, the founding ideologue of the Syrian and Iraqi Baath parties, was caught up in this stream of intellectual poison. The results can be seen to this day. The Baath party, according to columnist David Brooks, writing in *The Weekly Standard* in November 2002, while inspired at its origins by Leninism, "is not quite like the Communist parties." Instead, he says, "It bears stronger resemblance to the Nazi party," based as it is on a Nazi-like doctrine of racial superiority.

Terrorism

Meanwhile, in Egypt, a schoolteacher named Hassan al-Banna was founding the Society of Muslim Brothers, the radical group behind so much Islamist terrorism in recent years. Banna created a paramilitary arm to the brotherhood, modeling it after the Nazi SS. As University of London professor Efraim Karsh writes in his 2006 volume *Islamic Imperialism*, "Banna was an unabashed admirer of Hitler and [Italian fascist leader Benito] Mussolini, who 'guided their peoples to unity, order, regeneration, power and glory.'" Following the examples of the Nazis and fascists, he was perhaps the Middle East's first modern synthesizer of the tactic of terror, the cult of death, and the lust for conquest. Banna wished, Karsh notes, "to inculcate [Egypt's young people] with the virtues of death and martyrdom in the quest of Allah's universal empire. 'Death is an art,' he famously wrote, 'and the most exquisite of arts when practiced by the skillful artist.'"

After Hitler's defeat, many of these erstwhile Hitler allies and enthusiasts found a new supporter and model in the Soviet Union. Despite Russia's current dislike of Islamic terrorism, particularly in Chechnya, the old Soviet state was a prime financial backer and trainer of terrorists in the Middle East. Opposed to the U.S. by that time, as well as to the U.K [United Kingdom] and Israel, these groups passed the Cold War decades in alliance with the Soviets. Many of their leaders spent time in Moscow and all appear to have stayed in close touch with Soviet operatives.

Many of the regimes and groups we now see as adversaries in the Middle East were once Nazi and Soviet allies. Their ha-

Casualties in the Major U.S. Wars of the Past 100 Years		
Conflict	Number of Americans Killed	Total Killed
World War I	117,465	19,769,102
World War II	418,500	72,389,700
Cold War	148,445	78,000,000 (estimate, including victims of political repression)
War on Terror (through 2007)	7,399 (including deaths from the September 11, 2001 terrorist attacks)	140,766 (estimate)
Statistics compiled by editor.		

tred of the United States is not a new thing. Earlier generations of their leaders were equally intent on our humiliation and defeat.

Finishing the Conflict

So what does all this history tell us about going forward in Iraq?

First might be a lesson of skepticism about resolution of the Israeli-Palestinian dispute as a key to stability in the region. Israel is the product of populations fleeing early 20th century Russian oppression and later German oppression, with no place willing to receive them after the mid-1920s. They moved into a post-Ottoman political vacuum under the supervision of British caretakers entirely incapable of reconciling the rising Jewish nationalism of the refugee newcomers with the rising Arab nationalism of many indigenous locals. Yet if this now eight-decades-old conflict were to go away tomorrow, the region's regimes of inadequate legitimacy would have to find a substitute. Opposition to Israel is useful, even necessary, for many of them and will remain so as long as they lack popular sovereignty.

Second, the conflict in Iraq is a life and death challenge to other regimes in the region, particularly Iran and Syria. Our success would be their catastrophic failure. They have responded accordingly. Our strategic planning should recognize their roles and give first priority to answering the question, How do we take them out of the Iraq war? Opening talks with them, as many have suggested, cannot in itself be enough. An American labor leader once said that, in high-stakes negotiations, to make the other side see the light it is sometimes necessary to make them feel the heat. Where is the heat here? What will burn through generations of political pathologies? Would it be encouraging opposition groups within Iran? Or military incursions into Syria? Or working with the Saudis to drive down oil prices, as was done with the Soviets—if, indeed, the Saudis want us to prevail in Iraq?

Third, we should fix in our minds that the current conflict is the latest and, if successfully resolved, the final stage in a hundred years war, which, while often global, has focused on the fallen empires of World War I. In the context of a century of war, the present episode could possibly be ended within a decade and still be short. In the other phases of this extended conflagration, victory came when our leaders proceeded with a sense of urgency. That sense of urgency is needed now. On the battlefield, [Abraham] Lincoln should be our example. When a general didn't deliver, he was replaced. From September 1862 to March 1864, Lincoln went through five commanders of the Army of the Potomac until he found in Ulysses Grant a senior officer who delivered results. We need results. We may not get a perfect resolution to the war, but we must get an acceptable one. After a century of struggle, the stakes are too high to give up.

A 100-Year Conflict

Finally, while recognizing that we are in the last stage of a 100-year conflict, we should not beguile ourselves into believing this is the war to end all major wars. Maybe it is, but maybe not. There is North Korea, of course. Even more serious could be a rising China. The China of today bears an unsettling resemblance to the rising Germany of the late 19th century. In both, a limited opening of the economic and political systems produced remarkable economic growth. In both, the enormous growth enabled military build-ups unimaginable in prior decades. In both, there was no increased openness in the making of foreign policy in keeping with their liberalization in the making of domestic policy. So each military establishment retained or retains largely unfettered sway. In Germany, the consequence was an assertiveness that blew apart the 19th-century international norms and produced the First World War. In China, who knows what will happen?

All of which underlines that a sense of urgency in Iraq and throughout the Middle East should be the order of the day. Challenges are following close behind Iraq and Iran. Among the many things that have broken our way during this hundred years war is that we could take on challenges one at a time. We should resolve to pass that gift to the next generation.

Periodical Bibliography

The following articles have been selected to supplement the diverse views presented in this chapter.

Kyle C. Beardesley, David M. Quinn, Bidisha Biswas, and Jonathan Wilkenfield — "Mediation Style and Crisis Outcomes," *Journal of Conflict Resolution*, February 2006.

The Economist — "Blessed Are the Peacemakers: Gerry Adams in Israel, Sinn Fein Exports Its Expertise in Conflict Resolution," September 9, 2006.

Fred Kaplan — "You Say You Want a Resolution," *Slate*, August 14, 2006.

Andrew Kydd — "Which Side Are You On? Bias, Credibility, and Mediation," *American Journal of Political Science*, October 2003.

Paul Magnusson — "A Grand Deal for the Trade Dispute," *Business Week*, May 16, 2003.

Newsweek — "A World of Peace and Prosperity," April 20, 2004.

K. Salzinger — "War Zone: Learning from Social Psychology," *Psychology Today*, May/June 2003.

Carsten Stahn — "Responsibility to Protect: Political Rhetoric or Emerging Legal Norm?" *The American Journal of International Law*, January 2007.

UN Chronicle — "Challenging Times Ahead for Peacekeeping Operations," June 2004.

Rosemary Zibert — "Getting an Early Start on Peace," *Time*, June 10, 2002.

Mortimer B. Zuckerman — "A Momentous Moment," *U.S. News & World Report*, October 31, 2004.

For Further Discussion

Chapter 1

1. Peter T. Coleman and Beth Fisher-Yoshida contend that conflict resolution can be effectively taught at any point during a person's life, but Anita Vestal and Nancy Aaron Jones argue that dispute resolution is best taught to children. What are the main disagreements between the two authors? What are the points upon which the authors concur?

2. The *Business Week Online* viewpoint presents online gaming as a powerful potential tool to teach conflict resolution tactics. What would be the main drawbacks of video games as a conflict resolution teaching tool?

3. Based on the viewpoints in the chapter, how important are conflict resolution techniques in preventing violence? What does Chuck Kormanski claim is the main cause of conflict?

Chapter 2

1. Jeffrey Krivis in the viewpoint by Dick Dahl contends that traditional lawyers can learn quite a bit from mediators that use conflict resolution to settle disagreements. Does he make a compelling argument? What are the main strengths and weaknesses of his case?

2. Karen L. Douglas is an officer in the U.S. Air Force who practices conflict resolution in her everyday work. Does her position make her essay more credible or does it prevent her from presenting a balanced view of alternative dispute resolution?

3. Sheila Nagaraj argues that private judges and alternative dispute resolution are often more effective than the tradi-

tional legal system, while Brad Spangler highlights some problems with private conflict resolution. Which author makes a more compelling argument? Why?

Chapter 3

1. Jeffrey P. Cohn highlights examples of the use of environmental conflict resolution. Why does Cohn believe that this form of conflict resolution is used by the federal government? Are his arguments persuasive?

2. E. Franklin Dukes criticizes some aspects of environmental conflict resolution, while Faye Anderson generally praises the practices. What are the main areas of disagreement between the two authors?

3. How serious are resource conflicts? What are the main examples that Isabelle Humphries presents to prove that these disagreements influence security and stability in the Middle East?

Chapter 4

1. Sonam Wangdu discusses how Tibetans have used conflict resolution practices in their effort to gain independence from China. Does Wangdu believe that peaceful conflict resolution will lead to Tibetan independence? Why or why not?

2. Mark J. Hovee argues that psychology can play an important role in resolving international conflicts and combating terrorism. Does his military service enhance the credibility of his arguments?

3. Juliet Johnson contends that diplomacy is very effective in settling international disputes, however, Clark S. Judge asserts that armed force can also be a successful way to resolve conflict. Which author has the most compelling argument and why?

Organizations to Contact

The editors have compiled the following list of organizations concerned with the issues debated in this book. The descriptions are derived from materials provided by the organizations. All have publications or information available for interested readers. The list was compiled on the date of publication of the present volume; the information provided here may change. Be aware that many organizations take several weeks or longer to respond to inquiries, so allow as much time as possible.

Association for Conflict Resolution (ACR)
5151 Wisconsin Ave. NW, Ste. 500, Washington, DC 20016
(202) 464-9700 • fax: (202) 464-9720
e-mail: membership@acrnet.org
Web site: www.acrnet.org

ACR was created in 2001 through the merger of the Academy of Family Mediators (AFM), the Conflict Resolution Education Network (CREnet), and the Society for Professionals in Dispute Resolution (SPIDR). The ACR has twenty-two chapters and six thousand members who are engaged in conflict resolution and mediation. It provides resources on conflict resolution and sponsors a variety of publications on dispute resolution, such as *Conflict Resolution Quarterly* and *ACResolution Magazine*.

Carnegie Endowment for International Peace
1779 Massachusetts Ave. NW, Washington, DC 20036
(202) 483-7600 • fax (202) 483-1840
e-mail: info@ceip.org
Web site: www.carnegieendowment.org

The Carnegie Endowment for International Peace is a non-profit research organization that concentrates on international affairs, foreign and trade policy, national security, globalization, nonproliferation and democratization. The endowment was founded in 1910 and it promotes conflict resolution as a means to enhance cooperation between nations and contribute to global stability. The endowment publishes the magazine *Foreign Policy*.

Carter Center
453 Freedom Pkwy., Atlanta, GA   30307
(800) 550-3560
e-mail: carterweb@emory.edu
Web site: www.cartercenter.org.

The Carter Center was founded in 1982 by former U.S. president Jimmy Carter and his wife, Rosalynn Carter. The center sponsors a variety of peace-building programs and alternative dispute resolution activities. The organization has conducted missions and operations in sixty-five countries, including activities such as election monitoring, human rights investigations, and conflict resolution activities. Among its publications are annual reports and educational materials available through its teacher resource center.

Center for Education Reform (CER)
1001 Connecticut Ave. NW, Ste. 24, Washington, DC   20036
(202) 822-9000 • fax (202) 822-5077
e-mail: cer@edreform.com
Web site: www.edreform.com

CER is a conservative group that was founded in 1993 to inform students, parents, and teachers about educational choices and opportunities. The grassroots organization promotes alternative education and charter schools. It publishes a variety of reports and offers an annual report that ranks schools on spending, graduation rates, school choice, and other factors.

Committee for Children
568 First Ave. S., Ste. 600, Seattle, WA   98104
(800) 634-4449 • fax (206) 438-6765
e-mail: dhowe@cfchildren.org
Web site: www.cfchildren.org

The Committee for Children formulates curricula and lesson plans for preschool, elementary, and junior high school students across the nation. The committee's programs are designed to use conflict resolution strategies and alternative-dispute techniques to prevent bullying and physical harassment, sexual abuse, and youth violence. The committee provides professional training for teachers and educators in addition to its publications and course materials.

Conflict Resolution Information Source (CRInfo)

University of Colorado, Campus Box 580
Boulder, CO   80309
(303) 492-1635 • fax: (303) 492-2154
Web site: www.crinfo.org

CRInfo is a collaborative venture between the University of Colorado and the William and Flora Hewitt Foundation. CRInfo is a linking organization that seeks to provide access to other conflict resolution groups and information on the Web so that the resources can be used to reduce conflict and violence. Its Web site provides links to a range of other groups and educational materials, including instruction for teachers to create their own conflict resolution textbooks.

Educators for Social Responsibility (ESR)

475 Riverside Dr., Room 550, New York, NY   10115
(212) 870-3318 • fax (212) 870-2464
e-mail: info@esrmetro.org
Web site: www.esrmetro.org

ESR is an organization that works to ensure that social responsibility is incorporated into the nation's educational system. ESR offers a variety of initiatives that promote alternative forms of conflict resolution in the classroom and among young people, including the Resolving Conflict Creatively Program (RCCP) and the Reading, Writing, Respect, and Resolution Project (the 4R's Project). The ESR also offers alternative dispute resolution services.

Environmental Defense Fund (EDF)
257 Park Ave. S., 17th Floor, New York, NY   10010
(212) 505-2100 • fax: (212) 505-2375
e-mail: info@environmentaldefense.org
Web site: www.environmentaldefense.org

The EDF is a nonprofit organization that was formed in 1967. It now has more than four hundred thousand members and is one of the leading environmental groups in the United States. The EDF attempts to integrate science, law, and economic considerations to form environmentally friendly policies to address the major ecological issues confronting the country. It supports alternative dispute resolution practices in environmental controversies.

Family Violence Prevention Fund
383 Rhode Island St., Ste. 304, San Francisco, CA   94103
(415) 252-8900 • fax: (415) 252-8991
e-mail: info@endabuse.org
Web site: www.endabuse.org

The Family Violence Prevention Fund seeks to prevent violence in the home and the broader community. It promotes conflict resolution strategies and techniques in order to lessen violence in the family, but it also provides services to those who are the victims of violence and abuse. The fund also lobbies legislatures to enact laws to protect women and children and it was instrumental in the passage of the 1994 Violence Against Women Act.

National Wildlife Federation (NWF)
11100 Wildlife Center Dr., Reston, VA   20190
(703) 438-6000
e-mail: McNitt@nwf.org
Web site: www.nwf.org.

The NWF is an organization that promotes environmental interests and ecology. The NWF specifically attempts to preserve wildlife for future generations. It has offices and affiliates in

213

forty-eight states and publishes an annual report on the state of the nation's environment. The NWF encourages alternative-dispute resolution in environmental areas as a way to protect natural spaces and wildlife.

Peace Learning Center (PLC)

6040 DeLong Rd., Indianapolis, IN 46254
(317) 327-7144 • fax: (317) 327-7312
e-mail: info@peacelearningcenter.org
Web site: www.peacelearningcenter.org.

The PLC was founded in 1997 to spread peace-building and conflict resolution strategies to both youths and adults. The center publishes a variety of alternative-dispute resolution materials, including videos, booklets, and training guides, and it sponsors training for teachers and youth professionals. It also conducts the Peace Learning Camp for youths every summer in Columbus, Indiana.

U.S. Institute for Environmental Conflict Resolution

130 S. Scott Ave., Tucson, AZ 85701
(520) 901-8501
e-mail: usiecr@ecr.gov
Web site: www.ecr.gov/ecr.

The U.S. Institute for Environmental Conflict Resolution was created by the U.S. Congress as a resource to help resolve disputes over the environment and natural resources. The institute uses alternative-dispute resolution practices so that parties can avoid legal proceedings. The institute's Web site provides an overview of conflict resolution strategies and details ongoing programs, as well as resources and training opportunities.

Bibliography of Books

Kevin Avruch   *Culture and Conflict Resolution.* Washington, DC: United States Institute of Peace Press, 1998.

Yaacov Bar-Siman-Tov   *From Conflict Resolution to Reconciliation.* New York: Oxford University Press, 2004.

Guy Ben-Porat   *Global Liberalism, Local Populism: Peace and Conflict in Israel/Palestine and Northern Ireland.* Syracuse, NY: Syracuse University Press, 2006.

Amy Benson Brown and Karen Poremski, eds.   *Roads to Reconciliation: Conflict and Dialogue in the Twenty-First Century.* Armonk, NY: M.E. Sharpe, 2005.

Manas Chatterji, Saul Arlosoroff, and Gauri Guha, eds.   *Conflict Management of Water Resources.* Aldershot, UK: Ashgate, 2002.

Sandra Cheldelin, Daniel Druckman, and Larissa Fast, eds.   *Conflict: From Analysis to Intervention.* New York: Continuum, 2003.

Chester A. Crocker, Fen Osler Hampson, and Pamela Aall, eds.   *Leashing the Dogs of War: Conflict Management in a Divided World.* Washington, DC: United States Institute of Peace Press, 2007.

E. Mark Cummings and Patrick Davies   *Children and Marital Conflict: The Impact of Family Dispute and Resolution.* New York: Guilford, 1994.

E. Franklin Dukes, Marina A. Piscolish, and John B. Stephens
Reaching for Higher Ground in Conflict Resolution: Tools for Powerful Groups and Communities. San Francisco: Jossey-Bass, 2000.

John T. Dunlop and Arnold M. Zack
Mediation and Arbitration of Employment Disputes. San Francisco: Jossey-Bass, 1997.

David J. Dunn
From Power Politics to Conflict Resolution: The Work of John W. Burton. New York: Palgrave Macmillan, 2004.

Robert F. Durant, Daniel J. Fiorino, and Rosemary O'Leary, eds.
Environmental Governance Reconsidered: Challenges, Choices, and Opportunities. Cambridge: Massachusetts Institute of Technology Press, 2004.

D.S. Elliott, B.A. Hamburg, and K.R. Williams, eds.
Violence in American Schools. New York: Cambridge University Press, 1998.

Bradley T. Erford
Transforming the School Counseling Profession. Upper Saddle River, NJ: Pearson/Merrill, 2007.

Erik A. Fisher and Steven W. Sharp
The Art of Managing Everyday Conflict: Understanding Emotions and Power Struggles. Westport, CT: Praeger, 2004.

Patricia Friedrich
Language, Negotiation and Peace: The Use of English in Conflict Resolution. New York: Continuum, 2007.

Cedric H. Grant and R. Mark Kirton
Governance, Conflict Analysis & Resolution. Miami, FL: Ian Randle, 2007.

Tom H. Hastings	*Nonviolent Response to Terrorism.* Jefferson, NC: McFarland, 2004.
Myra Warren Isenhart and Michael Spangle	*Collaborative Approaches to Resolving Conflict.* Thousand Oaks, CA: Sage, 2000.
Libor Jansky and Juha I. Uitto, eds.	*Enhancing Participation and Governance in Water Resources Management: Conventional Approaches and Information Technology.* New York: United Nations University Press, 2005.
Tricia S. Jones and Randy Compton, eds.	*Kids Working It Out: Strategies and Stories for Making Peace in Our Schools.* San Francisco: Jossey-Bass, 2003.
Graham Kemp and Douglas P. Fry, eds.	*Keeping the Peace: Conflict Resolution and Peaceful Societies Around the World.* New York: Routledge, 2004.
Michelle LeBaron	*Bridging Troubled Waters: Conflict Resolution from the Heart.* San Francisco: Jossey-Bass, 2002.
Michelle LeBaron and Venashri Pillay, eds.	*Conflict Across Cultures: A Unique Experience of Bridging Differences.* Boston: Intercultural, 2006.
Melinda Lincoln	*Conflict Resolution Communication: Patterns Promoting Peaceful Schools.* Lanham, MD: Scarecrow, 2002.
Marick F. Masters and Robert R. Albright	*The Complete Guide to Conflict Resolution in the Workplace.* New York: AMACOM, 2002.

Kieran McEvoy and Tim Newburn, eds. — *Criminology, Conflict Resolution and Restorative Justice.* New York: Palgrave Macmillan, 2002.

Edward Newman and Oliver Richmond, eds. — *Challenges to Peacebuilding: Managing Spoilers During Conflict Resolution.* New York: United Nations University Press, 2006.

F. Ugboaja Ohaegbulam — *U.S. Policy in Postcolonial Africa: Four Case Studies in Conflict Resolution.* New York: Peter Lang, 2004.

John D. Orme — *The Paradox of Peace: Leaders, Decisions, and Conflict Resolution.* New York: Palgrave Macmillan, 2004.

Barry H. Steiner — *Collective Preventive Diplomacy: A Study in International Conflict Management.* Albany: State University of New York Press, 2004.

William L. Ury, ed. — *Must We Fight?: From the Battlefield to the Schoolyard, a New Perspective on Violent Conflict and Its Prevention.* San Francisco: Jossey-Bass, 2002.

Ernest E. Uwazie, ed. — *Conflict Resolution and Peace Education in Africa.* Lanham, MD: Lexington, 2002.

Peter Wallensteen — *Understanding Conflict Resolution: War, Peace and the Global System.* Thousand Oaks, CA: Sage, 2002.

Barbara Walter — *Committing to Peace: The Successful Settlement of Civil Wars.* Princeton, NJ: Princeton University Press, 2002.

Marc Weller and Stefan Wolff, eds. *Autonomy, Self-Governance and Conflict Resolution: Innovative Approaches to Institutional Design in Divided Societies.* New York: Routledge, 2005.

James L. Wescoat Jr., and Gilbert F. White *Water for Life: Water Management and Environmental Policy.* New York: Cambridge University Press, 2003.

Edyth J. Wheeler *Conflict Resolution in Early Childhood: Helping Children Understand and Resolve Conflicts.* Upper Saddle River, NJ: Pearson/Merrill Prentice-Hall, 2004.

Index